Susi Prescott lived in Sydney with her husband and four children, teaching French and writing freelance for sport and outdoor adventure publications before the release of her first novel, *The Astrolabe*, in 2005. Two years later she set off overseas to work as a language educator in Nepal and Rwanda, finally settling in Arequipa, Peru. She visits Australia regularly.

www.susiprescott.com
www.elohimarequipa.org

Praise for *Where Hummingbirds Dance*

'Courageous, beautifully written, understated ... a book that remains with you, and an inspiration for women of all ages to pursue their dreams and create some hope in a world of conflict.' **– award-winning author Susanne Gervay**

'Susi Prescott has a unique, surprising and discerning eye. Her companionable honesty, her joy, and her spirited discourse make for much learning and laughter.' **– Janet Fennell, author, writing teacher, librarian**

'A balanced view of a brave and generous woman immersed in the reality of Peru's underprivileged. Compassionate, funny and exciting.' **– Patricia Roberts, renowned poet and Tai Chi instructor**

Where HUMMINGBIRDS *Dance*

SUSI PRESCOTT

XOUM PUBLISHING

Sydney

In this true account of events as I have experienced them, some have been telescoped for the sake of the narrative, while all names have been changed except those of Rosa, Patricia … and Jack the family dog.

 XOUM

First published in Australia by Xoum in 2017

Xoum Publishing
PO Box Q324, QVB Post Office,
NSW 1230, Australia
www.xoum.com.au

ISBN 978-1-925143-35-5 (print)
ISBN 978-1-925143-36-2 (digital)

Cataloguing-in-publication data is available from the National Library of Australia

Cover design by Xou Creative, www.xoucreative.com.au

Papers used by Xoum Publishing are natural, recyclable products made from wood grown in sustainable forests. The manufacturing processes conform to the environmental regulations of the country of origin.

Pasado que no ha sido amansado con palabras
no es memoria, es acechanza.
A past untamed by words is not memory,
it is an ambush.

Laura Restrepo, *Demasiados héroes*

To everyone I met on the way,
especially Pattie, who taught me Tai Chi

PROLOGUE

I sit beneath green shadecloth at a table festooned with crêpe paper. Behind me, a painted sheet has been fastened to the wall, adorned with red, blue, green and yellow letters. On the cement patio, two hundred and fifty raven-haired children gather in their class groups: from tiny three year olds in pigtails and pocketed aprons to senior primary students, some in school uniforms, worn but neat, others in old tracksuits. I grin and wave as ebony eyes wide with excitement catch mine, and smiles light up radiant faces burned dark by harsh desert wind and sun.

Beyond the open school gate, a drab wasteland sprawls over arid hills dotted with half-built shacks and stones piled into makeshift walls. Between them, parched valleys sag under heaps of refuse; plastic bags spilling their rotting contents beneath the relentless sun. I look away from the dust and desolation to mighty El Misti, the still-active volcano with a personality of his own. His perfect cone rises to almost 6000 metres as he sits, marooned among his wasted foothills, watching the voracious illegal settlements clawing their way ever higher into his ravines.

The microphone crackles into life and a female voice instructs the children to take their places and prepare for my sixtieth birthday celebration. Over the following hour I watch, a queen upon my throne, as the children give short speeches and present me with their hand-made cards. They recite poems, sing songs and perform folkloric dances in costume, until finally, they bring out a huge cake. In the local tradition I plunge my face into it, hands behind my back, and resurface, doing my best to lick off the sweet cocoa while continuing to breathe. Luckily, a serviette appears as the torta is carried off to be cut into hundreds of pieces.

Children and teachers alike line up to give me a kiss and a wish. Starting with kindergarten, I kneel as tiny warm arms encircle my neck with shy murmurs, 'I love you, Mees Soosi'. I stand as I progress to the primary children and crouch down so little cheeks touch mine, 'Thank you for such fun English classes'. I straighten for hugs from the tallest and the teachers, 'I have learned so much from your training sessions. May God bless you for all you have done for us'. Any age-induced twinges fade as I bask in over two hundred and fifty cuddles.

Standing by the new classrooms built with funds raised from a network of generous supporters, I deliver a speech of thanks in careful Spanish. The audience listens attentively; children, teachers and mothers, many with babies in colourful blankets slung over their backs. When I finish, they applaud, and as I smile at them, my thoughts drift off to when I turned fifty, in another existence as a settled, married French teacher living on Sydney's North Shore. Today, I've just given an address in a newly-learned language at Colegio Elohim, a school on the dusty outskirts of a remote Andean town where I've lived for the past six years. How on earth did this happen?

CHAPTER 1

A decade earlier

Wouldn't be dead for quids!' I said, raising a glass of champagne. I sat on the deck of Mosman Rowing Club with my husband Richard and our four children: Katy, twenty-one, Peter, Lisa, and Rachel, all mid- to late-teens. We touched flutes and sipped, sitting back to watch the glittering blue water become silver in the setting sun, the silence broken only by clinks from the riggings of sleek yachts at anchor. We were enjoying a family moment before the official start of the centenary birthday bash we'd organised to celebrate Richard and I turning fifty within a few weeks of each other.

Exclamations and laughter rang out as the guests began to arrive, many of whom we'd known since university, having all married at about the same time and raised families together. They'd come armed with donations to the Fred Hollows Foundation instead of gifts, and we'd asked them to wear glasses in keeping with the evening's 'sight' theme. The range of eyewear had people falling about as they recognised each other. Bug eyes with waving antennae, open and shut models for applying makeup when age blurred things, swirly plastic lenses and half-masks, and Dame Edna Opera House numbers. I'd donned a curly black wig streaked with pink over my light brown hair with a pair of Harry Potter glasses, while Richard had framed his blue eyes with heavily-rimmed Austin Powers specs topped by a helicopter cap with propeller.

Ringing a bell at the end of each course of dinner, we asked people to move around so everyone could mingle. We blew out the ten candles on our cream mocha birthday cake, and as the slices arrived at each table, I stood and tapped my glass with a spoon.

'Congratulations, you've donated over $6000 this evening!' I said to claps and cheers. Waiting once again for silence, I went on, 'And now, dear captive audience, I present my specially-composed birthday poem.

'One hundred years between us!
Glory be, but what a shock!
It's enough to fog your glasses,
and make your false teeth rot ...'

Ten or so stanzas on came the final couplet,

'Our mid-age adventure has barely begun,
We'll do it all, together, and won't it be fun!'

Not two years later, my husband Richard was gone. My marriage hadn't been as safe, nor my planned future as rosy, as I'd thought.

We'd had our first and last meeting with a counsellor the day before he left. She listened to us for a while, then broke off and said, 'You came, apparently, seeking help to stay together, but from what I'm hearing you need the strength to part. Your relationship has become toxic.'

I felt as if I'd swallowed a brick. Floating in the sick silence was the truth which had emerged not long after our marriage at twenty-three, and hovered ever since. The opposites that had initially attracted us had an underside which had developed into a repetitive pattern of conflict. I yelled, Richard clammed up; his silence frustrated me, my noise appalled him; and despite my self-flagellation, nothing much changed over the years. I organised all the school and leisure activities for the children, a busy family social life, and frequent travel. These afforded precious moments and memories; but rather than solve the problems, they dragged me into a manic schedule of commitments which left me tired, irritable and impatient. A confident high-achiever on the outside, on the inside I knew how my anger hurt those I loved most in the world. My self-esteem plummeted as I wailed after my outbursts, 'I'm so sorry!

Couldn't we just forget it and go back to normal?'

'Until the next time,' Richard would respond quietly.

And now, finally, his dry lips brushed my cheek and he whispered, 'Be brave,' before walking out of my life.

At dawn the next day I stood at the bedroom window watching the frangipani tree take on its colours in the emerging daylight. An image two decades old appeared of our oldest daughter Katy, aged three, in an apple-green dress, sitting beside her dad on the low outside wall. Their backs to me, the pair surveyed several tied bundles of weeds that were ready for collection after the weekend's gardening. Katy's soft fair waves danced as she swung her legs and turned her little face up to his, asking, 'When will the garbage truck come?'

He smiled at her and answered, 'Tomorrow morning.'

'Can we wait for it?'

'Okay.'

As I stared at the same wall, now much higher and part of an enclosed courtyard, Richard's words from the day before returned. 'Be brave.' A flame of defiance surged within me. I had two choices. I could stay in Sydney, clinging to the raft of my former life ... or I could follow another path.

My mind hurtled backwards to bedtime stories with my father, his English actor's voice enthralling me with tales of travels as a young Royal Naval officer in the last flush of the British Empire; or reading from books ... Rudyard Kipling, set in the fevered jungle nights of colonial India, and legends of Pegasus the winged horse and the terrible Minotaur. Next, I was twelve, in a stuffy school assembly hall, watching slides shown by visiting missionaries of their work in the outback as my imagination lifted me up and away into another world of intense heat, stunted eucalypts and red dust beneath endless blue sky. Then my thoughts lurched forward into a fantasised future, and I saw a single, strong, independent woman in Africa, or India – I wasn't sure which – in a wide-brimmed hat and sandals, scooping out rice for hungry families; or sitting on the dirt in a grass hut with a class of skinny children. A pioneer helping the needy, speaking their language, even giving the odd TV interview on the job when CNN or BBC World braved the journey to visit ...

Susi, have you completely lost your mind? Your husband left you twelve hours ago. What are you thinking?

I crumpled on the window ledge, my head in my hands.

The ensuing weeks blurred together in a series of theatrical episodes through which I stumbled; tripping,

8

falling, and picking myself up again with the steadfast help of others. On that first afternoon, neighbourhood girlfriends rallied with wine and embraces; days later in the ladies' change room at the local pool I dissolved into tears and several half-naked fellow swimmers rushed to my aid. At home, my younger daughters Lisa and Rachel cooked meals and brought me endless cups of tea. When they went for their first evening with Richard at his rented flat, I opened a bottle of wine and watched *Under the Tuscan Sun*, weeping loud, long and messy. The following morning, nursing a blinding headache, I told myself this could not continue and signed up for a jazz ballet class on the 'dinner with Dad' night. In the same week, I joined a local group and began to learn the basics of meditation.

Support came from everywhere … schoolmates I hadn't seen for years, work colleagues, family and close friends, acquaintances I hardly knew. All gave their own special comfort in person, on email, by phone, from next door and around the world. One offered counselling, and with her, I entered a whole new world. Two mornings a week, we sat on a verandah amid grevillea and bottlebrush, cicadas drunk with heat roaring above us as we exposed and explored the turbulence surging through me. I did tests which categorised my personality, and discovered that my defects and strengths fitted a certain profile. At this, I felt a bit better.

★

By the time I turned fifty-two, Richard and I had been separated for ten weeks and I was walking in Tasmania with a group of friends. Loneliness plodded with me in the rainforest mud, padded alongside me through stands of beech, and pushed me up and over huge boulders in clammy fog. On the hot sunny afternoon of my birthday, I left my companions in the walkers' hut and scrambled up a rocky slope to a view of red waratahs, yellow boronia and white ti tree beneath ancient rock outcrops. I screamed some furious expletives into the silence, then calmed down, telling myself I could wallow in loss and bitterness, or welcome freedom and adventure.

On the way back, I stripped and rinsed my clothes in an icy clear stream, then slid in, gasping and splashing, before clambering onto a rock to stretch out and dry in the sun. An hour later, skin tingling and dressed more or less cleanly, I returned to the tiny wooden walkers' hut. There I found a plank-hewn table adorned with a packet-mix cheesecake and a musical candle. Everyone gathered round to sing 'Happy Birthday' and I cut the cake into fourteen pieces. As we clinked our enamel mugs, one of my companions said, 'Susi, no matter where you end up on your birthday from now on, you'll always have a family to celebrate with.'

CHAPTER 2

On April Fools' Day, a few months after the trip to Tasmania, I travelled to Peru for five weeks' trekking in a small group. We followed the Inca Trail to Machu Picchu, and for our final ten days headed to the sierra mountain range of Ausangate, twelve hours by rattling bus southeast of Cusco. The organisers of this second walk had asked us to distribute educational supplies, and we'd all agreed enthusiastically.

The first morning, we followed our donkey team slowly upwards through fields of beans, oats and potatoes, inhaling deeply as the altitude began to cut our breath. Past mud huts, ancient stone walls and herds of alpacas and llamas, we wandered into the domain of the indigenous people of the high Andes. Children walked with us, holding our hands, singing and laughing in their rubber sandals, skirts or track pants, worn jackets and knitted beanies. At the first school we visited, a colourful crowd poured from a cluster of mud-brick buildings in the middle of barren, windswept slopes. The teachers herded them into a yard, where they lined up to listen patiently to speeches of welcome. With my smattering of phrase-book Spanish, I could only manage 'Muchas gracias' and a couple of other words which they politely applauded. We then got down to the business of handing out books, pencils, crayons, sharpeners and erasers. Moving from child to child, I was struck by their natural beauty, high cheekbones, large eyes and lovely skin, olive though roughened by the extreme alpine weather.

The trek took us through a landscape of harsh, unforgiving beauty. Slopes of purplish-brown, dusted with green; streams rushing down wide valleys; and turquoise lakes brooding crystal clear. Always near, the mighty peaks of Ausangate loomed, their snow blinding in the morning sunshine, menacing in the bone-chilling sleet of afternoon. Passes of shale and scree at 5200 metres took every ounce of strength and left us gasping, choking with tears of exhaustion. Avalanches exploded from icy, churned glaciers and, one afternoon, the wind howled so fiercely it threatened to lift our tent. I cowered inside with my companion, trying to grab the soaking nylon and hold it down, our yells bringing the porters out into the storm to readjust the guy ropes. On clear nights the temperature dropped to minus fifteen degrees, the inky sky filling with spectacular stars.

We climbed higher to areas too isolated for a village, yet locals would appear from nowhere. More than once, as I organised myself in the tent, I'd turn to see six or seven pairs of eyes peering in. Outside, an entire family would be waiting – a proud man wearing the traditional beanie with ear flaps, colourful rug over his shoulders; his wife in a woollen blouse, multi-layered skirt and long dark plaits, often carrying a sleeping baby in a blanket on her back; plus children of various ages, every one a small replica of the parents.

One freezing morning at our highest camping site, I left the trekkers' breakfast tent replete and snug in my hooded down jacket, fleece tracksuit, gloves and boots, to find a little boy standing on the icy ground outside. He wore sandals, a pair of pyjama pants and a worn knitted cardigan. He gazed up at me from under a battered brimmed hat, his face solemn, his cracked lips unmoving. Kneeling down on the frost, I remembered the right Spanish words to ask him his name.

His reply came as barely a murmur in my ear, 'Salvador.'

Our tour guide had been watching and fetched some books and pencils. I handed them over to the boy and he wrapped his arms carefully around them, a gleam of pleasure lighting his deep brown eyes. He shivered as a stiff breeze stirred. I reached out to hug him close, inhaling his scent of woodfire and soil. Squinting up at the snowy mountain range, I felt again that flicker of defiant optimism. There in the Peruvian Andes, I made up my mind to leave my old life and head out into a new world, wherever the path might take me.

The path took me first to Nepal, a logical place to start as my Sydney college had a connection with a charity that ran children's villages and schools there. I requested long service leave and as soon as Rachel finished her final exams, I boarded a plane to Kathmandu. Over two weeks I hiked in the foothills of the soaring Himalaya along paths where Buddhist prayer flags scattered their messages to the winds and prayer wheels clattered and spun.

For three months after the trek, I travelled to schools around the country, taking student classes and instructing teachers in English methodology. The five-day residential course I conducted brought together participants from colleges all over Nepal; talented poets, published authors, dancers, singers and musicians, who happened to spend their working hours giving lessons in classrooms. They paired off as instructed to play card games, bingo, snakes and ladders, make flashcards, sing songs, and launch into acting and role play; even making Australian frog jelly cups and Vegemite sandwiches to study how to follow recipes.

At a ceremony to mark the end of the training conference, the headmaster presented me with a small golden statue of Saraswati, the Hindu goddess of knowledge.

'Susan came from far away and over this week she has spent every days and evenings with you teachers. She has been sharing her knowledge and giving her all. She has single-handedly prepared and conducted five days of many instructions which has been entertaining, informative and very unforgettable.'

I grasped my goddess. I'd taken a blind leap into the unknown and a new phase in my life had begun.

Back in Sydney, neighbours helped set up a massive garage sale in our front garden, with all proceeds going to Nepal. Katy, now married, returned home to assist Rachel and Lisa as they cleaned out all their junk and ransacked the treasures my son Peter had left behind when he moved to London. Over one long day, everything was sold, last of all the old backgammon set made in China, which we off-loaded to a group of laughing tourists to take back to Beijing. I stood in the chill of sunset surrounded by empty shelves and cleared trestle tables and wondered where my new life would take me next. I knew it wasn't back to teaching French in Sydney.

On the trekking trip in Peru, I had visited the city of Arequipa, an hour's flight southeast of Lima and situated by a river running through a fertile valley in the middle of the desert. One sunny Sunday morning, watching children patting and splashing the water of the fountain of the main square, the Plaza de Armas, I'd heard a whisper, 'You could live here.' Such fanciful notions had occurred to me on various trips over the years with Richard and the children, particularly in Provence and Burgundy, but they were immediately dismissed as ridiculous by my common sense. This time, it couldn't come up with any valid obstacles and since that day a plan had been percolating at the back of my mind. I would find a job and travel to Peru for at least twelve months, a prospect which terrified and excited me in equal measures.

I enrolled in an intensive Spanish course at Sydney University and sent an email to an English language institute in Arequipa. Before allowing myself too much time to think about it, I delivered a term's notice resigning my teaching position after fifteen years' service, further de-cluttered the house, and sold the seven-seater people mover. I invited Katy and her husband to move in as caretakers, living there with Lisa, who was working for a vet, and Rachel, about to embark on a degree in education. Only a single bed with faded sheets and an old doona remained for me in the small spare room. I'd backed myself into a corner. I hadn't received a response from Peru but had lost ownership of the family home and committed myself to going, by default.

Still avoiding the question of what exactly I was planning to do next, I reinstated my maiden name on all official documents, including an updated passport and a brand new divorce certificate. The lawyers finalised a settlement: a fifty-fifty split suggested by Richard in which he kept his business interests and I got the house and the modest inheritance left to me by my mother. I figured that with careful management I had enough for the moment.

Next, I next took a surprising detour to the remote hills of southwest Rwanda where I lived for three months in a cement hut without electricity or running water. Dodging downpours, I slipped and slid two kilometres up a mud path each day, carrying in my backpack hand-drawn flashcards and a battery-operated cassette player wrapped in a waterproof plastic bag. In an isolated clay-brick school, I taught French and English to wide-eyed children squashed into classrooms with dirt floors and windows with no glass. The training workshops I conducted for the shy, respectful teachers initially left them stunned; but we persevered, and they learned how to create sets of resources and find ways to use them in their own lessons. At the end of the final session, I watched the last young woman set out on foot to cover the several kilometres to her home, a vision of grace in a vibrant print outfit with her precious package of materials balanced upon her turban. I allowed myself a discreet air punch. Yes! It seemed that the workshops, in French on this occasion, had been understood and appreciated. Another gamble had paid off.

For three months, I became part of a subsistence culture still fundamentally connected to the land. Sitting outside my house at the end of each day, sipping a ration of fiery local banana rum, I'd watch clouds bank against a darkening sky over patchworked slopes and valleys framed by the red and black beans of coffee trees. Listening intently, I'd wait for the silence to yield sounds floating on the cooling air. A baby's cry, a child's laugh, their mother calling; birds, goats, cows; somewhere an axe striking on wood; and from everywhere, the sound of bare feet thudding on packed mud.

I returned to Sydney as a visitor in my own home, a situation I had knowingly created, so I now had little choice but to prepare for Peru. Still no word had arrived from the English institute in Arequipa, so I emailed them to see if they remembered me. Days later, I received a reply: 'We are expecting you for the first day of classes in September. You will need to obtain a business visa in your country to begin working with us.'

Help! In just three weeks! Did I want to do this so soon? Seeing I'd approached them in the first place, I could hardly back out now. The trips to Nepal and Rwanda had been short, and the prospect of a whole year away was something entirely different. Since that freezing morning in the high sierra of Peru when I'd met Salvador and made my decision, the looming challenge had sliced into my insides and turned them to water every single time I thought of it.

At the Peruvian Consulate-General in Sydney, I presented my documentation to the handsome young man at the counter. He checked it over, glanced around the empty office, and announced in perfect American-English, 'Things seem quiet today, so I can process this immediately.' He jotted down my mobile number and ushered me out to the lift. 'Why don't you go for a coffee and wait till I call you?'

I emerged through the glass doors into the dappled sunlight of Clarence Street and strolled to a nearby café. So far, so good. As I took the last mouthful of a cappuccino, he rang. My passport awaited, stamped with a 'Business Visa', ready for my Peruvian adventure.

CHAPTER 3

I hugged Katy in the passenger drop-off area of Mascot Airport, gulped down tears, and waved as she drove off. On the departures board, I located the flight to Buenos Aires via Auckland, where I'd connect to Lima and then Arequipa. Beside it blazed a word – 'Cancelled'.

A hot flush of panic surged from my knees to my throat. I waylaid an airport official who told me, 'The refreshment truck ran into the plane.'

'In Argentina?' The chaos of South America had erupted before I'd even left Australia.

'No, here in Sydney, this morning.'

I flew as far as New Zealand, and that evening, in a luxurious hotel paid for by the airline, I ate dinner with a young señora still weepy at leaving her Australian husband for a few weeks to visit her family. Picturing my girls, just three hours' flight away, I murmured, 'I suppose it could be worse.'

It got a lot worse. Anxious queues snaked around the counters at Auckland airport the next morning as exasperated señoritas re-ticketed over a hundred flights to Buenos Aires, twenty-four hours late. A shrill voice assured me that, 'Of course, all will be automatically re-scheduled for BA–Lima and on to Arequipa.' This did not happen, as I found out some twenty hours later from more exasperated señoritas at Buenos Aires airport and, even later, at Lima … by which time I felt too tired to care, and just longed to curl up somewhere and sleep forever.

The plane finally touched down in the outskirts of Arequipa at daybreak, seventy-two hours after I'd left Australia. Emerging from the plane's back door, I drew my fleece close, inhaled the sharp, dry chill and descended the steps into the gloom. I collected my backpack, found a middle-aged taxista with a friendly face, and greeted him with my best 'Buenos días', showing him my hostel address. I had written it down, not trusting my two-week intensive course to produce 'one hundred and twenty-five' in spoken Spanish after three days in planes, hotels and airports.

Conversational niceties drying up after 'Muy bonito Arequipa', I smiled and nodded in the rear-vision mirror at the driver's commentary as the small yellow taxi raced down wide thoroughfares lined with a jumble of dusty shacks, adobe shops and cement buildings under construction. The streets narrowed as we reached the town centre and I recognised the Plaza de Armas with its graceful stone arches, irrigated grass and elaborate fountain, where early tourists and street sellers already wandered among the palm trees. Half a block further on, with a cheerful smile and saying something which might have meant 'farewell and best of luck', the taxista deposited me outside Los Andes, a nineteenth-century British Georgian mansion that had been converted into a hostel.

Hoisting on my pack, I plodded up the steps, breathing hard, feeling the altitude of over 2300 metres. Pressing a buzzer beside a heavy iron grille, I heard a loud click as it unlocked. I pushed through and it swung shut behind me with a clang that echoed up a second staircase. Reaching the welcome desk and gazing blearily around at wide, airy passages painted in pastels, I gave my name to the receptionist. She greeted me with a warm 'Bienvenida Señora Soosan', evidently unconcerned that I'd arrived some thirty-five hours late. She checked me in and helped me up to a room overlooking the street with large windows through which the morning sun poured onto the floor, waxed to a shine.

'Anything you need, I am just downstairs,' she said with a smile as she left, closing the door softly behind her.

I heaved off my load and my boots. The window looked onto the plaza and the double white spires of the Spanish cathedral behind which El Misti rose, his arid folds and valleys a pattern of light and shade against a blue sky. I calculated that my girls would be asleep in bed and my throat constricted. What did I think I was doing? I remembered the fantasies which had seduced me. From the comfort of home, it had seemed a brilliant idea; living and teaching in Peru. Distant country, colourful culture, new language. And twelve months, not just three, the next step after Nepal and Rwanda. At the end of the experience I'd emerge triumphant, having left behind the charred ruins of my old life. Arequipa had ticked all my dream boxes.

I collapsed onto the bed fully clothed and fell into a fitful doze. The roar of the plane engines still throbbed in my ears as images whirled of a busy young family two decades earlier; babies, toddlers, birthdays, picnics, zoo visits, home theatrics, kids' meals, bedtime stories … Richard nodding off and losing the plot mid-sentence … 'That's not right, Daddy!' an indignant little voice ringing out.

A strident blast from a car horn startled me out of my slumber, but within moments my lids became heavy again and I drifted off to see my desk, red teacher's diary filled with lesson plans beside a pile of school permission slips; and on the fridge, the family spreadsheet logging our daily activities, surrounded by notices and photos held on by magnets.

I tried to force my eyes open, but before me appeared my mother, drinking tea in our back room as shrieks and laughter came from the garden.

'Make the most of it, Susi,' she was saying, 'it passes in a flash.'

I woke fully. The shrieks and laughter were coming from the street outside. I was lying in a stream of sunshine in a hotel room that smelt of floor polish, half a world away from my home, my children and their father. I got up and peered out of the window at a group of uniformed students racing to school, calling out to each other over the traffic's din.

The following morning, feeling slightly better after a good night's sleep, I emerged into a racket of cars, motor bikes, music and voices. Dodging the traffic, I found my way down pavements lined with stone façades to the institute to report for work. It occupied an old Spanish colonial residence, with original cupolas and patios hidden behind a high wall built in the local white volcanic stone. The ubiquitous material gave the town its name of La Ciudad Blanca, the White City.

Arriving at the institute, I entered a tranquil courtyard shaded by a jacaranda. At the director's office, a woman in her forties with long black hair rose to greet me in perfect American-English, 'Hi there, Susan, I'm so pleased to see you at last. I rang your hostel – what a dreadful trip you've had. Please, take a seat.'

By the third minute of our interview, I realised I had

seriously misunderstood the nature of the work.

'We offer English classes for young adults and children,' the director was explaining, 'from 7 am until 9.15 pm. A full-time workload is four ninety-minute sessions a day, plus Saturday mornings. Your timetable will change every month according to enrolments. Your salary will be 2200 soles a month, and annual holiday is four weeks.'

I smiled weakly. This sounded like my years in adult education back in Sydney. I recalled setting off twice a week at 5 pm, leaving my under-fives, usually all screaming, with a babysitter, to teach French night classes. In those days, I endured the timetable because it suited my needs, but as soon as Rachel had followed her older siblings to kindergarten, I found a proper job in a school, with decent, daylight hours matching my children's, plus paid holidays and regular benefits.

I stared, unseeing, into the director's face, as I began to realise that, having given up a full-time college job with fifteen years' seniority in Sydney, I now faced six hours' of teaching a day, probably until after dark, plus three hours on Saturday mornings, all for roughly $5 an hour, and a month's paid holiday if I survived twelve. Furthermore, I'd be speaking English most of the time instead of the Spanish I needed to improve.

'We are pleased to have you here,' the director went on. 'A native English speaker. We teach American-English and our students have considerable trouble with their Spanish intonation and accent.'

'Are most Peruvians of Spanish descent?' I asked.

'Oh,' she said with a laugh, 'we're all *mestizos*, mixtures, originally European, I suppose, but a melting pot of racial influences, even though we all speak castellano.'

This was the local name for South American Spanish.

'Everyone has been through Peru. Spaniards, Italians, British, French, Africans, Chinese, Japanese … although Arequipa is provincial, and here people tend to be *mestizo* or Indian, or various degrees in between. It's in Lima and on the coast you see much more variety.'

'What proportion is indigenous?' I asked, careful not to use the word she had.

'About a third are pure.' Again my first-world politically-correct sensitivities cringed. 'But only five million or so still speak Quechua. That's only seventeen per cent of the population.'

My eyes widened. 'But isn't Quechua the language of the ancient Incas?'

'The tourist industry promotes pride in the history and culture of the Incas, but that's about as far as it goes. Most of their living descendants, the Indians, who want to get anywhere, hide their roots and speak a fractured sort of Spanish, even with their kids. They see that as the way to break into the middle class.'

I sat silent as I digested all this.

'Now, Susan, we will have to get your immigration application underway.'

'Oh, that's already done,' I said, taking out my passport and turning to my 'Business Visa'.

The director glanced at it and smiled. 'This simply allows you to sign a contract for paid employment. Once you have done that, the application for residency must be submitted.' She handed back my passport. 'I'm afraid it will be a long and tedious process, but without it, you won't be able to work with us.'

I swallowed, remembering the plush, empty office of the Peruvian Consulate-General in Sydney, the cappuccino in the café next door, the reassuring metallic click of the visa stamp. No wonder it had all been so easy.

After the interview, I had an afternoon sleep before venturing out to a tourist pub on the Plaza de Armas. I planned to indulge in the Happy Hour deal of two for the price of one on the renowned pisco sour – lemon and sweet syrup frothed up in egg white, ice and bitters, with a liberal dose of Peru's national spirit. Yet, far from cheering me up, the experience rapidly descended into an Unhappy Hour. What I had discovered that morning at the institute had shaken me and I found myself sinking into damaging self-talk about impulsiveness, ignorance, rashness and, basically, idiocy. Around me, backpackers shouted in an excited babble of languages, straining to hear each other over the Latin music.

Walking home across the Plaza de Armas, I saw a girl of about sixteen crouched on the grimy pavement offering caramels to passers-by.

'Cuatro por un sol, Señora,' she called out to me, four for one sol. I fumbled in my pocket and pressed some coins into her cold hand. Peering into the faded patterned blanket over her shoulder, I saw a tiny baby asleep. His mother reached over to give me my sweets, but I shook my head and leaned forward to hug her, upsetting her bag all over the pavement. Before I could stop her, she was on her knees picking them up, her small frame bent beneath the weight on her back. I tried to help, muttering apologies, but she smiled and said, 'No importa, Señora.'

I walked on, feeling ludicrous. Having just spent six months getting my hands dirty in Nepal and Rwanda, I wanted to continue in the same vein here, to at least try to make a difference to these child-mothers on the streets. I wanted to learn their language, get out among them, understand their reality. Instead, I had signed up to teach English to privileged students with ambitious parents. They didn't need my services – they could pay a local for those. Nevertheless, pride would not let me give up so soon.

CHAPTER 4

My next expedition was down Ayacucho, the long, straight thoroughfare that led west out from the parks and flower-filled plazas of the established centre of town. Traffic raced past, tyres slapping the cobbled road surface, only to screech to a halt further down the road in a snarl of blaring horns. On an island at the centre of a busy intersection, cheerful women called out from behind their mobile stands; anything on wheels from converted prams to bicycles, displaying large plastic jugs of porridge. I presumed they'd been up before dawn preparing it. Children had come too, sleeping babies or laughing toddlers, in woven rugs slung over their mothers' backs. Amid the fumes, they poured out oats, and local quinua and kiwicha cereals into glasses for passing workers, some heading for the market or a building site, others suited and formal, on their way to the office. Between customers, glasses were washed in buckets of water on the pavement.

The footpath widened at Puente Grau, an ancient arched stone bridge spanning the Rio Chili rushing over rocks far below. Turning the corner, I spotted a modern, low building which housed an indoor swimming pool, part of a tract of land with basket- and volley-ball courts, an athletics field, tennis complex, manicured flower beds, and shaded paths beside the river. At the entrance, an elderly uniformed man stood under a sign, 'Club Internacional de Arequipa'.

In my search for a pool, I had come across the city's oldest established family and sporting 'club' – exclusive, and, I guessed, expensive. Used to being able to set out for a run anywhere in Sydney, I had already discovered that here in Arequipa, cobbled streets, narrow slippery footpaths, pollution and chaotic traffic made walking hard enough, and I imagined that jogging would be physically and culturally near impossible. So I took a deep breath and approached the guard on duty.

'Buenos días. Could you explain ...?' With hand signs, smiles and nervous repetitions, I eventually grasped the necessary information and found the office. There, armed with my Spanish dictionary and helped by patient staff, I completed some forms and handed over payment plus a photo. A few days later, with my own membership card, I began training – slowly, at an elevation higher than the summit of Mt Kosciuszko – and gradually eased into a routine of physical exercise and mental relaxation in a tranquil setting.

★

'Good morning everyone!'

Standing before my first class at the institute, I opened the class roll. I frowned as I read.

Cárdenas Meza, Herbert Jesús

Galdos Mendoza, Lucía Stefanie

Rodríguez Portilla, María Cecilia

Valdivia Espinoza, Juan Carlos …

Each student had four names.

I raised my eyes to survey the room full of neatly-groomed young Peruvian adults, observing me from behind their desks.

'Let's check attendance, shall we?' I said, and began stumbling through the list, mispronouncing every syllable, as the students politely corrected me. Finally reaching the end, I closed the roll and said as slowly and clearly as I could, 'I understand the given names; but why two family names?'

A girl raised her hand. 'Teacher, one is from father and one from mother.'

After a week of bewilderment, I pleaded, 'Choose just two. First and last. And please, do not change them.' It proved hard enough to read and pronounce even these, let alone remember them, for five different classes. I just began to master it all by the end of the month, in time to lose the groups and start all over again, with long lists of new challenges to get my head and tongue around.

'So, Teacher, what are the rules of when to use the pluperfect in English?' asked an earnest young man a few days later, his pen poised as I fumbled through the text to find the page. I found the detailed explanation of grammar in my own language tiresome, and suspected that someone else's efforts at doing so would be far better than mine.

'If you turn to page twenty-six, you'll find the rule. Now, let's try to put it into practice with some pair conversation.'

They looked blank until a few reluctantly turned to their neighbours. Most of them had not understood, and I had by now realised that my Australian accent caused them real difficulty. So I tried again, this time imitating the American movies, so they would recognise the sounds. I stressed my 'r' and came out with 'pairrr', and tried 'cahnverrrsation' instead of 'conversation' … and they all moved to face their partners.

I smothered a grin, thinking of my father's BBC accent. Sorry, Dad.

In one of my earliest afternoon lessons, what sounded like a scatter bomb exploded somewhere nearby, springing me off my feet. None of the students turned a hair. 'What on earth was that?' I squeaked.

'Oh, it's a virgin's feast day,' someone said.

'A virgin? You mean there's more than one Virgin Mary?'

'There are dozens,' came the reply, and various voices chimed in, 'Virgen de Chapi, Virgen de la Candelaria, Virgen de Fátima, Virgen de las Mercedes, Virgen de Guadalupe, Virgen de la Ascención ...'

'Which one has a festival today?'

Nobody could remember. After class I asked in the staff room and learned that districts all over Peru have their own virgins, blending their local Andean culture with the religion introduced by the Catholic Spanish missionaries in the sixteenth century.

'Our local virgin here in Arequipa,' continued my informant, 'is la Virgen de Chapi. She wears a wide-brimmed straw hat. It protects her from the desert sun.'

I grinned. 'And the fireworks?'

'All part of the celebrations. Dawn, morning, afternoon, dusk, midnight ... and the car alarms and dogs always join in too.'

The view from the top floors of the institute afforded some of the best moments of the teaching day. I could gaze down upon white curved rooftops, cluttered with junk, and the stone courtyards of colonial Arequipa; over her parks and plazas, and out to her three mighty volcanoes soaring skyward not twenty kilometres beyond. El Misti in the middle, the Chachani range to the west, and Picchu Picchu to the east, its lumps and bumps resembling, with imagination, a woman lying on her back.

Walking home one night, I smelled deep-frying fat as I neared one of the chicken and chips joints so popular with the locals and tourists alike. At a table in the fluorescent-lit interior I spotted four obese local children in private school uniforms with their parents, all tucking into enormous platters of fried eggs, chicken and chips. Just in front of me on the pavement outside, stood a small boy and girl, no more than eight, ragged and skinny, their straight black hair matted and unkempt. They made their way into the restaurant and sidled silently over to the table. Each one held out a packet of sweets for sale. Every member of the family glanced at them, turned away, and continued eating.

I marched into the shop and ordered two chicken hamburgers. Giving one to each of the selling children, I sat them down on the step in the entrance and smiled, saying what I hoped were the correct words and gesturing them to eat. They glanced uncertainly down the street, opened their bags and took a bite each, folded the rest away carefully and stood up again.

'Gracias, Señora,' they whispered, staring at the pavement before trudging off. It dawned on me that a parent was probably lurking nearby, and that, rather than help, I had probably caused them trouble.

Every morning before classes, I went to the club. I discovered the gym, and one day as I came downstairs after a session, a loud wave of Latin music hit me, just like the beats which rang out all over town from shops, cars, vans and buses. I followed it and found an auditorium full of middle-aged women leaping around while a young instructor wiggled and strutted his stuff. And I mean wiggled. I joined on the spot, discovered Emilio, and began dancing for my life. Feeling like an uncoordinated mess of arms, legs, bust and bottom, I kept at it, class after class, buoyed by the music and the encouragement of my companions. 'How do you do it?' I found the words to ask one day, having made not a jot of progress trying to simultaneously shake my shoulders and wobble my torso.

'Easy,' replied the girls, showing me the basic move. From then on, I practised diligently, unconcerned which parts of my intimate anatomy shuddered and shook. Emilio seemed to be able to shimmy his top while his bottom didn't move at all … and he could also do it the other way round, in a 'booty shake' which turned my legs to jelly and left me gaping.

CHAPTER 5

In between teaching classes, I made two trips to the Arequipa Immigration Office to complete the first stage of the residency application. I relied entirely on the human resources secretary, who spoke no English, and a kind work colleague who came along to translate. The documents were finally dispatched to Lima, with assurances that the paperwork would eventually arrive in Arica, Chile, a day's bus trip away, where I'd collect the visa. I settled down for the long wait.

At the first staff meeting, with one hundred other teachers in a hall, I listened with my limited comprehension to what sounded like the same sort of content I'd regularly sat through at my Sydney college; only now in Spanish, so even less enthralling. Glancing round, I spotted a tall Scandinavian woman of around sixty, her face glum, absently stroking her flaxen bun. She caught my eye, moved over to sit next to me and said in accented English in a husky smoker's voice, 'I've heard all this before. I'm Greta, by the way.' As soon as we could escape, we headed for a pub to share our doubts about exactly what we'd let ourselves in for.

'I've been travelling to South America in my holidays for eighteen years,' Greta told me.

'As a tourist?'

'As a volunteer. The past ten I've come to Arequipa to help in a refuge for kids of street sellers and beggars. To try and give them safe shelter while their parents are working. I've got a not-for-profit at home to raise funds.'

'Wow. Do you have any family?'

'Just my son, and he's grown up now. So I can sub-let my flat, and as soon as my primary school breaks up for the three-week Christmas holiday, I'm onto the plane, out of the Swedish winter. Usually I can organise a bit longer away by working extra during the year.'

'So why are you at the institute?'

'I always get a casual job to help pay the bills when I'm here ... but with all this fuss about immigration, I don't think I'll stick with it. The pay's better, but the hassle of getting the visa isn't worth it for the short time I'll be staying. I'll just pick up something informal and get paid in cash.'

'Oh. I've already begun the visa application. No way out for me now.' I sounded flippant, but I didn't feel it.

★

I blame the pisco for the dream I had that night.

As I dozed off, I saw a little girl, tottering alone in the sunlight along the deck of a huge passenger liner as it pitched above the dark, heaving depths. The ship lurched, throwing her to her knees. She grabbed at the vertical rail as she swept past ... but she couldn't hold on and the force flung her tiny body out into the void to hurtle downwards into the churning greedy water below with barely a splash ...

'No!' I gasped aloud, neither asleep nor awake. 'That can't have happened ... the child is me, and I'm still alive ...'

She reappeared, surging unsteadily forth on short, sturdy legs, persistent in her perilous journey, having escaped from the daycare centre in the ship's stern. This time she finally made it to the prow, stumbling forward, crying out as her chubby little arms reached for her mother. The young woman turned, screamed, 'Oh my God! Susi!' and shot out of her deckchair, her husband following close behind.

I jolted awake, remembering the place and the date ... SS *Orsova*, 1958, travelling from England to Australia. A homeward journey for Mum, having refused to endure another northern winter; for Dad, emigration to a new country at fifty, as a commander just retired from the British Navy; and for my older brother and me, nine and four and both born overseas, the beginning of a new life.

I just had time to reflect that my career at the ship crèche must have ended that day, when another vision flashed before my eyes. Four bulky British Austins with 'Police' signs on top, parked along a tree-lined street, and helmetted men in uniforms with capes, striding, heads down, searching up and down hedged laneways and over a green lawn in front of a Tudor-style house. My mother huddled on the steps weeping in my father's arms. My seven-year-old brother clanging the bell of a parked fire truck, glinting red in the afternoon sunlight among the black police cars.

Next it was pitch dark, biting cold … a motorist's headlights pick up a tiny girl toddling along the side of the bitumen … me again, heading north on the main Maidstone-London road, aged just two.

'Wake up! You're dreaming!' I heard myself yelling, and struggled into a sitting position in my bed. But the little girl was still vivid, babbling, 'A white puppy, Mummy! And … and ladies with sparkles and long black hair … they gave me yummy hot soup!' Mum had told me the story when I was in my teens; how I'd slipped away and remained missing for the entire afternoon and half of the night until the driver had spotted me and rung emergency. She thought I'd followed the dog into a gypsy camp.

Now, wide awake in the Arequipeñan pre-dawn chill, I shuddered as I reflected what could have happened, and wondered ... why did I set off again, leaving warmth and food, to end up wandering on the main road in the middle of the night? I felt sure that the little girl had been trying to return home from her adventure, a strong wanderlust struggling against an equally powerful yearning for the safety of her family ... as it had continued to do all my life.

Decades later, I had loved ones of my own whom I had cherished and raised ... but now, thousands of kilometres separated us. I had to find a new path to follow, in the hope it would eventually lead me back to them.

'I must change course.'

The following morning, still groggy, I thought of the dreams, of my new Swedish friend Greta, of the chicken and chips joint, and of my job at the institute. I picked up the photo I kept beside my bed of Salvador, taken up in the high Andes, and contemplated his quizzical gaze as he clung onto his precious books and pencils. I made my decision. Exploiting my exotic status as a native English-speaking gringa, I negotiated a part-time load, something previously unheard of at the institute. Just two sessions every afternoon plus Saturday mornings, beginning the following month. Now I'd have time to find the children who really needed me.

I moved to a quiet, cheaper room in the hostel, sharing facilities, at the back of the building, with a view over a neighbouring church and out to the desert hills. Like a nun in a cell, I made myself comfortable, for, after two unsuccessful attempts, I sensed it would take some time to find a flat of my own.

My neighbouring 'nuns' included Anja, from Denmark, in her mid-thirties, who arrived the week after me to take up a position at a local German-run orphanage as a social worker. On our first meeting, she said to me, 'No hablo inglés, sólo castellano!' and from that day, I believed she spoke no English and stumbled to speak to her in Peruvian Spanish. This did wonders for my skills in the local language, as we became friends, the locals often mistaking us for gringa sisters, with our fair hair and blue eyes, despite the differences in our ages, languages, heights and countries of origin. I also met Jen, from the US, twenty-five, the same age as my daughter Katy, fluent in Spanish and visiting Arequipa for a few months, eager to find volunteer work.

I slipped into a routine, heading with Anja to dance

at the club at 7 am each day, returning to the hostel for breakfast, before spending the morning studying in my room. I had arrived in Arequipa fluent in French and equipped with what I remembered from my two-week intensive Spanish course. Both are romance languages, I reasoned, so it shouldn't be too hard to pick up. After a week of trying French on the locals and meeting with blank stares, I realised the error in this assumption. Out and about every day, I struggled with every linguistic situation imaginable in castellano; after which, in the privacy of my room, I searched through my grammar book to try to find out what I should have said. I continued to work through tapes and notes, knowing as a language teacher that pure slog was the only way to improve. But I hadn't counted on the negative influences of French, and in fact had to un-learn pronunciation and structures that had been second nature for decades. I felt sure that tackling another language over the age of fifty didn't help things, either.

One day the ATM in the supermarket refused to deliver money on the debit card into which my salary was paid. A slapstick comedy followed, due entirely to my alarming linguistic inadequacy. In the administration office at the institute, it was decided the problem was faulty ID documentation, caused by Immigration in Lima. I jogged down to the bank with a staff member, to hear the señorita scanning my account on her computer screen announce that the error had nothing to do with immigration … someone had simply typed my ID number incorrectly, and the bank would need to send a photocopy of my passport to Lima and back to rectify the situation. This would take at least four weeks.

All activity then ceased for the three-hour lunch break, but when I returned to the office mid-afternoon I was greeted with a complete turnaround, and astonishing new information. The supermarket had swiped my card three times, exhausting my available cash. A simple mathematical and mechanical error. A kind retail assistant accompanied me the following day to the offices of the debit card provider and sorted the whole thing out in rapid castellano. As I walked home, it struck me that, until my Spanish improved beyond the six-year-old level of my current vocabulary and grammar, I would fall victim to every fantastic tale anyone cared to pluck out of the air to suit their needs.

My gaffes were spectacular. Get just one letter wrong and I'd be brushing my horse instead of my hair; putting on my boats instead of my boots; at the delicatessen asking for soap instead of ham; in a conversation about furniture, provoking wide grins by confusing drawers with balls, of the anatomical kind. A serious effort at work fell apart when small female dogs were substituted for inspectors; grave insult risked as old people were labelled dirty; and I would, still, never dare try to say comb for fear of coming out with penis.

Each afternoon, I set out to work down baked city streets, jostling overheated locals for a place on the shady side. Arriving early in the empty classroom, hot and sweating, I kicked off my shoes to cool my bare feet on the tiled floor before the students entered.

The desert sun burned like an electric bar heater, but the shade brought shivers, and sunset at 6 pm meant a sharp night chill and the need for a warm jacket. From everywhere came warnings of the dangerous levels of radiation in Arequipa due to latitude, altitude, depleted ozone layer and terrain. The parched climate caused additional effects; first, 'crusty desert nose', hunks of hard − I have to say it − snot, just waiting to be pulled out, often causing bleeding. Second, dry skin at a level previously unimaginable, and even more wrinkles, despite slathering on locally-made Andean creams. Finally, my curls disappeared, leaving my hair limp and straight, not at all helped by the hat usually pulled down over it. I tried growing it, cutting it, but no matter what I did, it just sat on my head like an upside-down cardboard box with flaps sticking out at right angles over my ears.

On the way back to the hostel after classes, making my way through the crowded plaza, past the cathedral spires lit up against the dark sky, I would detour to ring home from a phone booth upstairs in a converted colonnade. Crouching over the telephone in bright light beneath an arched stone roof, I'd chat with Katy, Lisa or Rachel, whoever was around in the late Sydney morning. I imagined them sitting at the kitchen table as they invariably said, 'Everything's okay, Mum, don't worry.' So I'd tell them my news, such as the evening Jen and I went out to the Plaza de Armas to meet Greta, armed with a blanket and some puzzles and toys to try to encourage children on the streets to visit her refuge.

'We sat on a bench,' I said, 'unpacking our things. It was freezing! One or two children came to watch us, and joined in, stacking building blocks, while Greta called out to others she already knew, to try and get them to come and play, and find out where their mums were working.'

'Mum, I can't believe you did that!' an exclamation crackled down the line.

'Only once, and I felt pathetic, shivering inside my hooded fleece jacket while these little kids didn't seem to notice the cold, putting their puzzles together under the street lamp. I don't know how Greta does it, turning out night after night, just trying to find them again.'

'Sounds amazing.' As I heard that utterance so indiscriminately favoured by the young, I wondered what they secretly thought about their middle-aged, middle-class mother's antics on the other side of the Pacific.

★

Around that time, I saw a photo on Facebook of all three daughters enjoying a backyard barbecue with a group of smiling companions. I peered closer, and recognised Richard with his new partner. I quickly clicked 'Escape'.

As more people and places entered my post-divorce life, I would use them in meditations of a parting of the ways between Richard and me. I'd visualise him walking, with his new love, into a nebulous beach sunset while I strode, alone and free, towards an exciting new existence. I struggled about where to position our friends and more particularly, our children, in this idyllic scene. Who was I trying to fool? I was still as jealous as hell. But then, I reminded myself, when they were with their father, I couldn't join them; and of course, it would be even worse, dealing with it at close range. I was better off far, far away. Thus my head would reason, but sometimes my heart just didn't want to listen.

CHAPTER 6

One morning almost three weeks after my arrival in Arequipa, I came downstairs to find Gisella at reception waving a leaflet. 'Señora Soosanita,' she said. 'You should go to this – it will be very wonderful to show you our food and music.'

'Mucho gusto,' I replied, knowing I'd used the wrong expression, and thinking how much worse my Peruvian Spanish must sound to her than her English did to me.

The leaflet featured a jovial face with a chef's hat and the words, Festi Glotón, Plaza Yanahuara, 14–16 de septiembre. A gluttony festival. Irresistible!

I woke just after dawn on Sunday September 16th to the sound of church bells, as the sky turned from light grey to blue. The sun shines in Arequipa from April to December, so event organisers don't spend any time, or money, on contingency plans in case of a wash-out. I hadn't seen a drop of rain since my arrival and

sometimes longed for Sydney's cleansing cloudbursts …
but not today.

Strolling down Ayacucho with only the occasional
passing yellow taxi, I crossed the bridge and walked
through a park shaded by trees. Before me appeared a
woman in a pink tracksuit, matching runners, cap and
sunglasses, with a pair of furry baby dolls on eight legs
pulling her in all directions. Each Schnauzer wore a
dress stretched over its canine body, and four pink plastic sandals. I didn't know whether to burst out laughing, or gasp in shock.

Up some steps I found a maze of cobbled laneways
lined with high white stone walls, spilling brilliant
red and purple bougainvillea over tall wooden doors.
Finding one ajar, I peeped down a passageway to a
shady courtyard full of potted greenery, and stairs leading up to a sunlit cupola roof bright with blooms; a
gem of colonial architecture, some four hundred years
old, with arches and thick, sturdy walls, hidden from
the outside world. I'd reached the ancient former village of Yanahuara, meaning in Quechua 'black knickers', once the red-light district of Arequipa, but now a
sought-after inner-city location. I decided immediately
that this was where I wanted to live.

I finally found the local plaza, with grass and flower
beds beneath palm trees around a central fountain.
Pansies bloomed in a riot of colours and I suddenly
thought of my dad and imagined him kneeling down

among them, turning the soil with his trowel. I remembered him pruning his roses, and carefully tying up the stems of his sweet peas on the wire trellis, decades ago in our Sydney backyard. Every year without fail, they came out in crimsons and mauves just in time for a scented bunch on Mum's birthday. My father spent most of his working life on board a ship, but once he retired to our house on its block, he never again expressed any desire to be near the sea, devoting every spare moment to his beloved garden.

He died of cancer in 1987, the same year baby Lisa arrived, and we farewelled him with a small private ceremony at a Sydney crematorium. He'd never been one for church services, always saying he'd had enough at naval college, where he'd been packed off aged fourteen. 'I do rather hope that we live on in the memories of others,' he once told me, with those vowels that more than a quarter century in Australia never touched. 'If someone thinks of me fondly one day after I've gone, then that's enough.'

It occurred to me that his wish had been granted more than once since my arrival on the South American continent.

From the arched lookout, I gazed over the town, and several kilometres beyond, where the outer suburbs gave way to a sprawl of squatter settlements, spreading upwards as far as the base of the vast volcano. I turned around to survey the festive square, its perimeter lined by shade-cloth kiosks set up as traditional kitchens and restaurants, in which costumed staff fried and stirred ingredients in huge pans, or vigorously rattled cocktail shakers. Thick bundles of electric wires weaved all over the ground to feed appliances, microphones and loud speakers pumping out salsa, as spicy aromas permeated to the hungry crowd.

With a repertoire by now of about fifty words of Spanish, and almost no knowledge of local culinary customs, I felt like an *idiota completa* peering into earthenware pots and metal trays, sniffing to guess their contents as cheerful vendors launched into enthusiastic patter I couldn't understand. Finding a dish of crackling pork which took me straight back to childhood Sunday roasts, I lost my nerve completely and resorted to pointing. The friendly señora served me a whopping helping on a polystyrene plate.

Searching around for a square centimetre of chair, wall or grass, I heard a male voice saying, 'Hola, Soosi!' and turned to see a handsome man with soft brown eyes and abundant wavy silver hair, who clearly knew me. 'Antonio, from the institute!' he continued in perfect American-English with a seductive inflection.

'Oh, yes, of course,' I replied, returning his smile, without the remotest idea who he might be, still overwhelmed by the bombardment of new names I couldn't even pronounce, let alone remember, since starting work.

'How are you settling into your classes?' he asked.

'Okay,' I lied, 'more or less.'

He glanced past me. Was he checking if I had come alone? In the pause that followed, something tingled in my stomach.

'I won't keep you from your meal,' he said, nodding at the dish balanced in my hand. 'Enjoy our food of Arequipa. Hasta mañana. See you tomorrow.'

Here we go again, I thought as I walked back from the Festi Glotón. My chest heaved and I physically squirmed as I remembered an evening at a Sydney pub about halfway through the previous year. Sitting in a dark corner, kissing a 'date', I'd heard a deep, 'Bonsoir Madame!' and glanced up, startled, to see a tall young man smirking at me. 'It's Steven. You taught me French in primary.' A particularly intelligent student I'd last seen aged eleven, had arrived to hang at the bar with friends, and come across his old teacher making out with someone equally ancient. The floor had shown no inclination to do the humane thing and swallow me, and the excruciating embarrassment of the moment perfectly summed up my year-long exposure to the

Sydney single social and internet dating scene, aged over fifty, after thirty years as part of a couple with four children.

I stared down unseeing as the cobbles of Yanahuara passed beneath my feet. Sure, at the time I'd enjoyed occasional moments of feeling attractive and desirable, adolescent even, but the baggage I was hauling along behind me, not to mention that of my partners, meant doomed encounters which had ended in three more if not heartbreaks, certainly emotional disturbances, over twelve months.

And now we have a handsome Peruvian to add to the list. I imagined another brief link in a long chain which would stretch to the end of my days.

Antonio simply smiled and greeted me in passing at the institute for the first few days after our meeting, until I found a postcard of Arequipa in my pigeonhole with a little message inviting me to watch a street festival with him one evening after work. In the end it didn't eventuate, so we simply went for a short stroll through town. As he pointed out landmarks with enthusiastic and knowledgeable commentary in his lovely accented English, I linked my arm through his and felt him tremble and then relax into a natural pace. He stood slender, about one head taller than me, and walked with a spring which matched my own.

The following Friday he asked me out to one of the myriad Chinese restaurants which have remained entrenched as part of the culture of Peru since contract labourers first brought the cuisine with them in the nineteenth century.

'Do you mind if we share?' he asked, 'I can't eat much all at once; ever since I was a child. But I get hungry often, and I always struggle to maintain weight.'

'What a wonderful problem,' I said and laughed, 'no wonder you're so slim.'

He told me he had been divorced for eight years and had two adult children, a son and a daughter. We discovered they were the same ages as Katy and Peter, as I gave the barest details possible of my recent history, and changed the subject as soon as I could. I asked him instead to explain to me the squatter settlements I had seen spreading around the town from the lookout at the Plaza Yanahuara on the day of the food fair.

'Ah,' he sighed, 'they are called *pueblos jovenes*, or "young towns", and they spring up as a result of what we call *invasiones*. Certain, shall we say, "unsavoury" individuals locate an expanse of desert wasteland and peg out "blocks" which they then "sell" illegally to rural folk who want to move to the city. In the dead of night on an organised date, fifty or more family groups from the mountains arrive in a convoy of battered vehicles, and get to work with plastic, canvas, matting, spades and hammers to erect rough shelters to prove their ownership. That's how these slums begin.'

'But isn't that illegal?' I asked.

'Of course. But who is going to remove these poor people once they have set up their homes? It would be a scandal beyond all proportion. There would be demonstrations and battles. The authorities, at any level, wouldn't dare … and so the "invaders" stay, and the person who sold them their lots becomes the leader of the community, the *dirigente*.'

Looking up from the spring roll on my plate, I thought of the parcels of property released on the outskirts of Sydney in ordered new allotments which people queue to buy.

'But who owns the land in the first place?'

'It's wasteland, desert. Nobody owns it before the invaders arrive and claim it to invest in their dream for a better future.'

I blinked, trying to imagine how the numerous members of a newly-arrived family survived the first weeks under a sheet of plastic in the middle of the desert.

We finished our meal, split the bill, and moved on to a karaoke bar, something I'd only experienced once when Richard and I had hired a machine for one of the kids' birthday parties. 'Everyone in Peru loves to sing, and we have much talent,' Antonio whispered proudly to me as we took our seats, and after watching two polished and confident acts, I had to agree. I croaked my way through 'My Guy', while he sang a Peruvian ballad in a lovely tenor voice. We took a taxi home and just before we reached my door, he drew me into his arms and kissed me. His warmth and tenderness made me wonder if perhaps this man would be different.

Later, in the hostel, I knocked on Jen's door with two cups of cocoa. 'How did it go?' she asked. Sitting on her bed I shared my uncertainties and hopes with a caring girlfriend less than half my age.

CHAPTER 7

Now working part-time with free mornings, I set about searching for voluntary work, ably assisted by Jen, with her fluent Spanish. By chance, I picked up a pamphlet in a travel agency and found a sentence inviting travellers to donate any unwanted clothes which would be sent on to Colegio Elohim, a school in the squatter slums of Arequipa. Jen found a phone number, rang it and two days later set off into the wild in the company of another volunteer. For a week I remained behind, trying to get my castellano up to speed, until one afternoon Jen announced, 'Tomorrow, you're coming with me.'

Early next morning, we boarded the battered grey combi. Fleets of these minivans, usually owned by private companies, run an exhaustive network of complex routes all over the city and surrounds competing with several thousand taxis to provide the main forms of communal transport in Arequipa. They have seats for about twenty and standing room for as many commuters as can be physically squashed inside; and while some vehicles are relatively new and well-maintained, this one had seen far better days. We each found a seat and fell into it as the combi took off, black exhaust belching, salsa blaring from the radio. I noticed several passengers crossing themselves, nervous, I supposed, given the crazy speed, until I realised it happened every time we passed a church.

We wound through the congested streets, our conductor, a young woman in jeans and jumper, calling out to stop the driver as she hauled open the door for passengers getting on or off, then pushed it shut again. The uniformed students and suited professionals gradually disembarked, and as we reached the dry limits of town, nylon tracksuits wedged in around us. From my seat I observed wind-roughened faces, many missing several teeth. An earthy smell intensified when they slammed the windows against choking dust as the asphalt road petered out.

We stopped, and the conductor, a slight girl, heaved at a rotund elderly lady to get her up the steps; a mama-cha, part of an older generation of women which still dressed traditionally. A black hat perched upon her head, thick grey braids snaking down her back, woollen stockings below full petticoats, she propelled her substantial behind onto the front seat, as a youngster dived off it. The combi crunched its gears and began to climb, and through the grimy window I saw piles of bricks and stones, half-dug foundations and one-room dwellings by the dirt road. We'd begun the grind up into the parched foothills of the volcano locally nicknamed its 'skirts'.

On a corner, a woman in jeans stirred bubbling pots on a coal fire. The combi slowed, the conductor leaping off to fetch two plastic plates loaded with meat, rice and potatoes. She balanced them on the dashboard in the sun, and I caught a whiff of spicy deep fry as we took off again, both dishes somehow staying put.

The van wound ever higher, past steep ravines, choked with rubbish hurled out in the baking sun. Inside the combi, heat turning fetid, it crossed my mind to leap up, shout to get off, and fall through the door into the open air, before jumping on the next vehicle out of there. Then through the bottoms I spotted Jen in her seat with a tiny girl on her lap, ribboned pigtails bobbing as she laughed. I pulled myself together, grateful to have my young companion to show me the way in the packed combi to the last stop, and whatever waited there.

★

By the time we got to the end of the line, only Jen and I remained on board. We climbed out into the dusty road, littered with garbage, building rubble, rusty tins, mongrels and their faeces. A pack of males snapped and growled at each other as they circled to take their turn and mount a cowering bitch with teats still enlarged from the last litter. I stared, recalling the fashion excesses I'd seen lavished upon the city counterparts of these mangy, half-starved creatures. We skirted around them and tried to focus straight ahead. In places, the unmistakable smell of human waste hung in the air.

Puffing uphill, we passed shacks made of blocks hacked out of volcanic rock, their tin roofs held down by stones, on plots surrounded by boulders heaped into piles. Some had neatly-swept dust yards strung with faded, fluttering colours – clothes drying in minutes under the desert sun. We came across a communal tap with several large plastic buckets lined up in front of it, waiting for the water truck. 'How could anybody even lift them, once they've been filled, let alone carry them home?' I gasped.

'I suppose the women do it,' Jen replied, watching as a mother with a baby tied on her back approached down a treacherous, steep track, with two empty jerry cans which she dumped in the queue. Jen spoke briefly to her and waved as she left. 'They do,' she whispered, 'and the water truck comes every third day, with a total weekly ration of eight buckets for cooking, cleaning and washing. It's supposedly fit to drink, but everybody has parasites.'

Plodding on up the stony track, I thought of the grim conditions of life in the mountains I'd witnessed trekking the Ausangate range, the stone huts at 4500 metres, with crops in the frozen soil and small flocks of sheep, minded all day by tiny shivering children like Salvador. In the shacks surrounding me lived people who had turned their backs on that tradition to take their chances in the desert outskirts of the city where, as Antonio had explained, at least the combi could take them to markets, hospitals and schools.

I tried to imagine the view on the first morning of the settlement I now walked through. A cluster of hopeful flimsy blue tents flapping forlornly in the breeze, clinging to the steep crumbling hillside – no water, no power, no shelter, nothing but hot, burning sun in the dry season, torrential rains in the wet, and, always, frigid night winds …

'We're here,' said Jen, breaking into my thoughts. At the top of a rise, we'd reached a wall painted with a map of the world. Young voices began singing on the other side, ringing out in the desert silence. Once they had finished, we pushed open the high metal gate and stepped into a small courtyard covered with green shadecloth, and brightly painted with numbers and words. At least one hundred children's faces, just like those I had seen in Ausangate eighteen months before, turned to us from a sea of ragged uniforms and street clothes. A woman stepped forward, wearing a neatly pressed trousers suit, and leather shoes free of dust. I glanced down at my scruffy pants and runners, and up again as a smiling, serene face, framed by long wavy black hair, leaned to kiss my cheek. She turned to the assembly and announced, 'Señorita Jen has brought a new visitor today.'

And so I found Rosa, and Colegio Elohim, in the slum of Héroes del Cenepa.

As an active young father, Antonio had taken his family on many expeditions into the city and its surrounds, and now he announced his intention to revisit all his old haunts with me on Sundays, our one full day off work. On our first outing, he called at my hostel in brilliant sunshine, waiting downstairs like a teenager visiting his girlfriend at residential college. With his local knowledge of combi routes, he knew exactly which one to catch. After half an hour we disembarked, the last passengers, into a little village square on the rural outskirts of town, with a church of white stone amid patterned gardens, its bell chiming out the last worshippers from morning mass. I had told him I enjoyed walking, so we found a path out to the cultivated terraces, ancient structures dating from the time of the Incas, and forged our way up and over pungent-smelling plots of onions, garlic and potatoes, greeting farmers crouching under straw hats, tending their crops. They stood up to watch us, and waved back, but they must have thought us *locos* – for nobody else in Arequipa would dream of marching through fields sown in the desert, least of all stop in the middle of a bean plantation under an olive tree for a picnic. I feared Antonio had risked ridicule for my sake.

As we ate our bread, avocadoes and ham, he sipped his beer and told me how he'd brought his son and daughter to the village often as they grew up. I remembered sitting with Richard on rocks in the Australian bush, watching our children paddle and splash in creeks so different from these springs which bubbled up and flowed through stone irrigation ditches, to disappear again beneath the sand. Surveying the dusty littered hills beyond the plantations, I felt homesickness wash over me as I left most of the talking to this man who shared my present, but not my past.

He explained the difference between the rural, traditional village nearby, and the squatter settlements like Héroes del Cenepa. Subterranean water had irrigated these fields and terraces for hundreds of years, and they all belonged, legally, to land-owning families. On the other side of town, he said, my combi journey out to Colegio Elohim tracked the transformation of the illegal slums into outer suburbs over the decades. The 'immigrants' arrived and laid claim to areas of parched wasteland, then over the years agitated in marches and demonstrations, led by their local leaders, the dirigentes, through the city streets, clamouring for power and water, paving and sanitation. Slowly, as their demands were met, the area transformed, and the slums were pushed further out, to the barren areas where newer arrivals settled. As he spoke I thought of my bumping journey out to the little desert school; in fact I was passing through recognisable zones of societal development.

'Are the dirigentes elected?' I asked.

Antonio pulled a face, 'Aye, Soosanita, slum politics have nothing to do with democracy. They are dangerous, corrupt individuals and the people know better than to cross them. Now. Enough of this serious talk. It's time for lunch.'

'But, we've just finished it,' I said, indicating the remains of the picnic.

'That was merely a snack,' Antonio said, jumping up and holding out his hand to me. 'Arequipeñans enjoy a substantial meal in the middle of the day.' We walked back across the terraces, eventually taking our seats on the shady wooden verandah of a small restaurant, packed with families at tables groaning with food.

★

The following Sunday we stayed in the town centre, wandering through the Plaza de Armas. Antonio nodded towards a group of men in worn clothes gathered under the palm trees, murmuring to me, 'They are waiting in case a farmer comes past searching for casual labour for the day. This is the known spot.' We walked towards the cathedral. 'The left tower was destroyed in the earthquake of June 2001. It crashed here, onto the plaza, at 3.30 in the afternoon. It's a miracle only a handful of people died.' I asked him where he'd been when it struck.

'In the market with my daughter. I'll never forget it; the earth began to move in waves as if we were balancing on the surface of the ocean. Apples, oranges, watermelons tumbling all over the place. People screaming. A group of us all held hands in a circle to try and stay upright. It stopped, and then started again, twice.'

'I couldn't even imagine how that would feel.'

'I hope you never find out. They were the longest minutes of my life.'

Far above us, angels and saints in pastels adorned the restored ceiling. 'How long did repairs take?'

'The tower was back in position within twelve months.'

We explored the Santa Catalina monastery, its alleys of former nuns' dwellings painted blue, dusty pink and yellow. As we climbed up steps into little alcoves and adjoining rooms, he explained that the sisters, from the highest echelons of Spanish colonial society, had enjoyed many luxuries and privileges in their secluded lives.

Whenever we walked down the pavement, he positioned himself protectively between me and the traffic as he continued with his commentary, opening up Arequipa to me through his eyes, his considerable knowledge, and his memories. When we finally returned to his rented room, he read me several verses he had been composing about our developing relationship. I seemed to have stumbled upon a Latin man who was romantic, charmingly-mannered, intelligent, sexy and available … and he even wrote me poetry.

As we explored over the weeks and months, I discovered a jumble of contrasts all jammed in on top of one another. Gorgeous old cupolas and heartless modern brickwork, graceful stone arches and drab, cold cement, pristine manicured lawns and littered pavements, charming cobbled laneways and clogged choking streets, irrigated green terraces and dusty construction sites. Several of the high white walls which lined the streets hid ugly surprises, as I discovered when we peered through a hole into a devastation of tumbled stones, broken timber and smashed glass, overgrown with weeds and covered in rubbish. 'Rats' nests,' said Antonio. 'While extended families squabble over inheritance for decades, the disputed family home falls into ruin.'

One evening we went to a retro disco, which played Latin music, and rock from the sixties and seventies. 'I am a roquero, not a salsero,' he announced firmly, and proved the point with wilder and wilder rock 'n roll antics as the night went on. We sat out the salsa brackets, and watched couples swinging and swaying, the women following the strong and sexy lead of their partners, who moved with complete confidence; one young man so much so that he didn't mind dancing with his girlfriend's bulky pink handbag slung over his arm so she could dip and turn unencumbered. I turned with a grin to point the comical sight out to Antonio, to find him watching me intently. He whispered earnestly how much he loved me, and poured more pisco into his glass from the jug he'd ordered. Neat or with water, it tasted awful to me in any form but a pisco sour, so I left all the drinking to him.

In October, enormous drapes of purple went up over some of the churches in town, and certain middle-aged women began wearing smocks of the same hue, with golden sashes. 'It is the month of El Señor de los Milagros, Lord of Miracles,' explained Antonio in Spanish which I had insisted we start speaking exclusively, made possible by his patience and expert tuition. 'At the end,' he continued, 'there is a procession. It would mean a lot to walk with you and give thanks for the miracle which brought us to each other from the opposite corners of the earth.' Having grown up a not particularly devout Anglican, since my separation I'd embraced Buddhist meditation in Sydney and Nepal, shared prayer with nuns in Rwanda, and now welcomed any ritual of faith, so I readily agreed.

The night finally arrived, and I walked slowly with Antonio, himself a 'lapsed' Catholic, mingling in the warm companionship of the crowd, cupping a hand over my candle flickering in the breeze, while a brass band paced beside us, playing from sheet music pinned to the backs of those in front. Up ahead, the robed brotherhood of the Church hierarchy staggered forward under the weight of the effigies of Jesus and Mary, stopping every few hundred metres to rest, chanting and praying, engulfed by clouds of incense.

'Who pays for all this?' I whispered.

'The cost is met by a wealthy middle-class family in the parish and it is a coveted honour to be selected.'

Afterwards, we sat in a huddled embrace in our fleece jackets at a trestle table, lit by lanterns, and sipped scalding Diana tea, sweet, milky, infused with cloves and cinnamon. We clinked to toast our love, while our motherly waitress refilled our china cups and smiled at us. I looked into his brown eyes and he held my gaze. 'I can read your whole life in them,' I said and smiled, 'they tell me everything. I can see the eager little boy you were, the father you became, the sadness, the joy, the intelligence, the love.'

A disarming grin radiated over his face. 'At university, our group of friends had a competition. The girls voted for the boys according to their best attributes. I didn't have a chance with my skinny legs, wonky teeth and crooked nose, but I won the eyes.'

I laughed. Yes, this man was different. Yet, as I began to feel myself falling, a voice somewhere deep inside nagged with worry, 'You're far away from home. Where can this possibly go? How else can it end but in heartbreak?'

CHAPTER 8

It didn't take me long to do exactly what I now criticise so much in gringos; march into Colegio Elohim and tell Rosa and the staff – in my then still appalling Spanish – exactly what they needed, and that I proposed to give it to them. Fortunately, what I had to offer did indeed happen to be just what they wanted; a program of English for the whole primary school, so they readily accepted, and I found my volunteer work. In November, Jen moved on from Peru, leaving me behind to give classes in Grades 3 to 6 three mornings a week, with my usual methods. I bought a CD player for singing, dance and movement, and with plentiful access to cheap photocopies and taping facilities all over town, I could easily make cards to use in conversation pairwork. To make myself understood I used my emerging castellano, some English, and a lot of mime and gestures, and from the start my students reacted eagerly.

★

Watching as the teachers brought unfailing enthusiasm to the difficult conditions, I asked Rosa about their salaries. She told me they came from Jimmy, a middle-aged member of a church in the US, where he lived with his younger Peruvian wife and their two children. In her family's home in Arequipa they'd established a dental clinic for underprivileged patients, and they had known Rosa for some years. She told me that Jimmy collected donations from his church in Colegio Elohim's name, which he channelled through his practice to her. He had visited the school several times over the years with groups of English-speaking gringos who always took a lot of photos. Rosa, unable to communicate with them, never found out who they were; but accepted that all this activity must be generating funds to help her pupils. Once the donations arrived in the Peruvian account, they were managed by Jimmy's in-laws; his wife's brother, mother, aunt and cousin, all members of the church mission in Arequipa, and all living in the house attached to the dental surgery.

'I have to cross town to the clinic each month,' said Rosa, 'to collect the $1000 Jimmy sends to pay the teachers' wages, but often the brother-in-law tells me there's not enough, and that they need it for the clinic. He even says that soon there will be no more funds for salaries. Es un poco difícil. Sometimes I think he enjoys making me beg,' she added.

I wondered at such apparent malice in someone who called himself a Christian.

Meanwhile, halting conversations with teachers and children in castellano during my initial months at the school gave me my first glimpses into the ugliness of life in the slums, particularly if you happened to be less than twelve years old. Rosa's wisdom and compassion shone through as she guided my initial, hesitant steps over a cultural minefield, in my stumbling endeavours to come to terms with the reality of the 'young towns' sprawling across the desert around the 'White City'. I pondered over what she told me and what I saw and heard, and tried to understand.

High in the mountains left behind by the parents or grandparents of our pupils when they came to settle outside Arequipa, even the poorest and most isolated village had its codes of conduct. The festival of the local virgin may have meant dances and processions and an alcoholic binge of fermented corn beer for a week, but after that, everyone had to get back to work in the fields for the sake of the food supply; a simple matter of survival. However, those beginning their new lives in these squatter settlements found themselves alone, flung out of that social network into a dry, dusty atmosphere of suspicion where no-one could be trusted. As soon as they could, after building their shack of volcanic stone, they put up a high wall around it with glass shards cemented into the top, and invariably adopted two or three half-starved mongrels as guard dogs; for anything left unprotected or not locked-up risked being stolen – concrete slabs, building tools, gas bottles, even clothes hanging out to dry. In no time, a corner store sprang up selling basic groceries … and, inevitably, a plentiful supply of cheap home-brewed spirits and beer to dull the pain as disillusionment set in.

With no other choice, they battled on, and they had babies. One after the other, thanks to culturally ingrained machismo which apparently equates virility with masculinity, and a superstitious fear of birth control on the part of both men and women. They lived in harrowing physical conditions, without the means to feed their offspring, nor much example from their own upbringing to follow in caring for them. Like their parents before them, they had little concept of children's rights – to protection and, most importantly, to an education, with access to the knowledge necessary to break the cycle of poverty and abuse.

I thought of Salvador and wondered if his family had remained in the frozen high Andes. If they'd joined the urban exodus, it was possible that somewhere, in a slum on the outskirts of Arequipa, or a smaller city like

Puno, or Cusco, this tragic sequence of events could, or had, in fact become his story.

I taught several key English phrases to my pupils which they parroted enthusiastically; although they grasped only the most basic concepts of comprehension and pronunciation. But then, I'd remind myself as I bumped back to town on the midday combi, the main bulk of their parents could neither read nor write in any language.

Back at the hostel I'd quickly prepare a 'safe' salad of peeled carrots and apples with cheese. As I'd already discovered, for all Arequipeñans, including my colleagues at the institute, lunch was the main meal of the day, an inexpensive menú of soup and a hot main course, served anywhere between 12 and 3 pm in small restaurants all over town or at home. Antonio always ate one, although he confessed to leaving most of the abundant potatoes and rice. I couldn't imagine eating any heavy meal, let alone a starchy one, in the middle of a working day, used to a more substantial dinner in the evening when I could relax. So I held stubbornly to my Australian habit of a light lunch, after which I'd change my dusty clothes for something more formal, and head to the institute for my two afternoon sessions.

Coming across Antonio between classes I returned

his suggestive smiles, relishing the excitement of our liaison, which was easy to keep private from the staff as we all rushed from room to room with little time for conversation. Focused firmly on enjoying the present, I tried not to think about betrayal … of my own family if I stayed, and of my lover if I didn't.

In the light just before day began, lost in my thoughts, I turned into Bolivar, a street running several blocks beside the high wall of Santa Catalina monastery. I was walking across the deserted city to the swimming pool for my early Saturday 6 am swim before children's classes at the institute.

All of a sudden, an iron grip from behind pushed hard against my windpipe. No time to react. *If I don't take a breath soon, I'm going to die, right here and now.* I felt a rough jacket against my throat, smelt its mustiness, and then a body pressed into mine from behind in a horribly intimate movement. The last thing I remembered, a man's soft voice, his mouth at my ear. Next, I was waking up in my bed at the hostel … *No, Wait. That's the monastery wall against the blue sky, high up above me. I'm not in bed, I'm lying flat on my back on the pavement. Oh my God!*

I got slowly to my feet, and crept, sick and shaking all over, back to the hostel. Gisella rushed from the front desk to help me crawl up the steps to collapse on my bed, where I burrowed into the blankets and cried. Some time later, after several cups of tea, I went to reception and phoned the director of the institute to explain why I couldn't teach that morning. Horrified, she told me to come in when I felt better, so someone could go with me to the tourist police. Next I rang Antonio to tell him what had happened. His voice and reaction seemed oddly unsympathetic, unfamiliar even, but I put it down to his surprise.

I duly ventured out with a work companion to report the incident; then, back at the hostel, a call came from Antonio at midday wondering why I hadn't been at work. The penny dropped; when I'd phoned him after the attack I had dialled the wrong number and spoken to a stranger. Now I stammered out what had happened and fifteen minutes later he arrived at the hostel, charged up the stairs to my room and sat in anguish on my bed, holding my hands and hugging me with tears in his eyes, whispering over and over again, 'Mi querida Soosanita.'

This would be my first inkling of the deep sense of responsibility he felt for me in his city where poverty blurs the boundary between right and wrong and engenders a perverse kind of racism. To the young thieves I was just a gringa with a backpack, a rich tourist, the perfect target to rob unseen from behind. Never mind leaving me lying unconscious in the street, with a burning sore throat which lasted for weeks; all for a threadbare towel, cap and goggles – oh, and my battered straw hat.

Antonio shepherded me to the market that same afternoon to buy replacements and get me used to being among crowds again. But he warned me, 'Mi amorcito, someone will always be watching you.'

I didn't tell anyone in Sydney about the assault, in case they ordered me to catch the first plane back. I had too much to lose to surrender to fear, having left my children, my home, my friends, my job and invested so much heartbreak, and hope, in this adventure. So I ditched wearing a backpack, and from then on my purse, mobile phone, and camera travelled in my commodious bra, stuck in where no-one would dare try and get at them without risking a punch in the nose. Anything else went into a plastic supermarket bag.

The hostel rang a taxi for me to go to the pool on Saturdays before children's classes, a major inconvenience as it often arrived late. Even so, at that hour of the morning, it seemed a safer option than walking.

CHAPTER 9

They must be moving house. Odd time to do it, 10 am on a Sunday morning.

Two young men pushed a battered-looking upright piano on trolley wheels along the pavement in the neighbourhood of San Telmo, Buenos Aires. I was spending a few days following a Christmas trek exploring the tranquil lakes, icy glaciers and mountains of Chilean and Argentinean Patagonia with a group of Australians.

Why have they stopped? The piano had been abandoned in the middle of the pavement, or so I thought, until one individual returned pushing a round stool, and sat at the keyboard. Four more arrived, wielding a violin, a cello, two concertinas and chairs upon which they settled themselves, spreading out sheet music over the pavement at their feet. Two vibrant chords burst out from the pianist, to be joined by the strings in a haunting, mournful melody, and finally the accordion player began squeezing out the unmistakable, pulsing rhythm of an Argentinean tango. Passers-by stopped to listen and within moments two had begun to dance, a man of about fifty and a young woman no more than twenty-five. They had not arrived together, so presumably did not know each other, yet her face transformed into a mask of agony and passion as she tossed her dark hair and flung her body back, secure in the strength of his hand firmly grasping her waist, locking her closely against his thigh. He swayed her back and forth with the intimate assurance and mastery of years of practice; slow, slow, quick, quick, slow; legs rotating and turning slowly, sensually, as they moved in a precise choreography over the cobbled street. As I watched, others joined them in a timeless Sunday morning tradition of this bohemian quarter of the Argentinean capital.

I wished I could have shared the moment with Antonio, but I had not even broached the subject of him accompanying me. He was an educated member of the professional middle class, but the cost of the trip, run from a first-world country for travellers on first-world salaries, was out of his league. Furthermore, I had simply 'told' the institute that I would be gone for a few extra days beyond the Christmas break, which I would make up upon my return; but I realised that Antonio needed his job too much to even dare to make such a suggestion.

Before I'd left Peru to join the trek, he'd given me

a card with a painted view across sunlit water from the shadows behind a half-open window. 'Remember me in those quiet moments as you gaze from your room over mountains and lakes,' he'd written, 'and know that I am thinking of you.'

Returning to Arequipa in January I found it transformed, the rainy season having arrived during my absence. Without fail, the sun shone only till midday, when the sky darkened, and fierce afternoon storms lashed the city. Roads flooded in minutes, spraying brown water into shops and all over pedestrians as the traffic thundered past, while armies of municipal employees in yellow raincoats with brooms swept rivers from one place to another. The volcano El Misti appeared at first light wearing his white poncho over his shoulders, which usually melted by noon, while Chachani and Picchu Picchu remained frozen.

I met Antonio and his son and daughter one evening over a pizza in town. Although I didn't understand all of the conversation, I felt welcomed. His son worked out of town while his daughter Nohémie lived with his ex-wife in the family home in the suburbs. As is so common in Peru, no legal settlement had followed his divorce and for the moment he claimed he needed little beyond living alone and in peace.

Neither Antonio not I ever mentioned the future. A fellow teacher at the institute once said to me, 'We Peruvians don't plan ahead like you Westerners do. We can't.'

'What did he mean?' I asked Antonio later. He looked at me and shook his head, saying simply, '*Sendero Luminoso.*' His eyes filled with tears as he told me of the twelve-year bloody insurgency of the Maoist guerilla group known as the Shining Path; of the indiscriminate torture and slaughter in Andean towns and villages in the deepest mountain regions by first the terrorists passing through, and then the army pursuing them.

'And the chaos in Lima,' he sighed. 'It was the Shining Path who invented the car bomb. My sister still tells how one explosion blew out the windows of her apartment, and then the aftershock sucked the shattered glass back in again, flinging it all over her tiny children. But in Arequipa, we were never touched. The leader Abimael Guzmán spared the town of his birth.'

As Antonio went on to describe the years after the terrorist insurgence, when inflation hit 1000 per cent as he and his wife struggled to feed and educate their son and daughter, I began to see the reasoning behind my colleague's comment about planning, and to suspect how sheltered my upbringing in Australia had been. I had certainly heard of the troubles back at the beginning of the eighties, but only taken enough notice to strike South America off my travel itinerary. I concentrated instead on a working holiday for Richard and me in Europe before settling in Sydney to have children in prosperity and peace.

'It's time to leave,' I said one morning upon opening the door of my hostel room after a night of persistent rain. I hitched up my pyjamas to wade through a clear, icy stream flowing swiftly over the tiles of the covered corridor to the communal bathroom.

Scanning the paper an hour later, I spotted a 'to-rent' notice. Gisella rang for me, and I walked to the address to meet the landlord, who showed me to the third floor. Taking in the airy kitchen and living room, bedroom and bathroom down the hall, I signed the lease at once. The following evening, in a downpour, a taxi dumped me and my bulging backpack at the door of my first-ever bachelor flat. On a busy street rather than a winding cobbled laneway, and certainly not with a flower-filled courtyard, it was nonetheless situated in Yanahuara, over the river beyond the mid-city mayhem, but still walking distance from it. I had found a home in the area I'd set my heart upon.

★

To walk from the apartment to the supermarket I had to cross the Avenida Ejercito. This 'Avenue of the Army' is the continuation of Ayacucho which links the city centre with the northwestern sprawl. The pavement heaves with people, strident horns deafen, fumes belch and asphyxiate as an unrelenting onslaught of vehicles struggles through endless traffic jams. The chaos doesn't discriminate; shuddering wrecks fight with the latest model sedans and hatchbacks, tico taxis battle combis and buses bursting with people. Traffic volume has long since outgrown this cobbled 'avenue'.

Crossing the Ejercito can be life-threatening. Only in a group can the attempt be made, in aggressive stance, arms up, facing the drivers, forcing them to slow to a stop, before crossing with a wide, grateful smile. In a stroke of luck on my first morning, I found a policewoman in tight khaki skirt, knee-high boots, and shiny black hair beneath a pert little hat. She blew her whistle and raised her hand – in patriotic red and white Peruvian gloves – to stop the traffic. 'Gracias, Señorita,' I called as I stepped off the kerb, aware that few of her male counterparts would have assisted a hapless pedestrian, preferring to lounge in the shade, only moving to harass buses trying to drop off and pick up passengers.

Some days later, I found an intersection with traffic lights and crossed with the flashing green man, but a turning car almost collected me and I realised that it was not facing a red arrow. Shaken, I reached the other side, where I spotted a teenage boy in his wheelchair on the corner. His legs crumpled and stunted, his body from the waist up strong from heaving and rotating his vehicle, he clattered down the steep kerb every time the lights turned red, weaving in between waiting cars, offering sweets for sale. Fishing them out of his bag, he passed them to motorists, deftly catching coins handed through windows; and all in time to manoeuvre himself up and out of the way before the traffic took off again in a cloud of exhaust. Whenever I dropped money into his cup and took a few caramels, his tranquil face would light up with a smile. Sometimes a girl in school uniform, presumably his sister, wheeled him to his chosen spot where she stayed for a while, before tenderly kissing his head and hurrying off to class.

When I told Antonio about the lad, his troubled eyes sought mine. 'In a town like Arequipa you can spend all your money on little people and hardly make a dent. You need a project to concentrate your fundraising and your energies.'

On a wet, miserable morning in late January, I arrived at Colegio Elohim to find Rosa sweeping water out through a door, and struggling to rearrange desks which had been piled in a corner to escape the daily inundations. The long school vacation, from Christmas to early March, matches the rainy season, but during January, Rosa and some of the staff continued the daily combi trek up to Cenepa, skidding in mud rather than dust, to conduct holiday reinforcement classes before midday and the onset of the downpours.

'Rosa, let me help,' I said, moving to pick up some chairs.

She put down her broom. 'Mees Soosi, please come with me.'

I followed her outside into the mud, and her two senior teachers, Yulissa and Sylvia, came out of the room next door to join us. They pointed up to the half-finished brick wall which sat on top of the two down-stairs classrooms. It had not progressed since I'd first seen it months before.

'We've run out of money,' Rosa said. 'Could you possibly help?'

There, shivering beneath a grey sky, staring at a pile of sodden bricks, I discovered my project.

'I need to know more if I'm to raise funds,' I replied. 'Why don't we all sit down and you tell me how the school began?'

We pulled a table and some chairs to the middle of the soaked cement classroom floor, and when we'd settled ourselves, Rosa began the story.

She studied education, then started work for an elderly gringo with connections to a British mission, teaching the children of poor 'immigrants' from the mountains in a rented stone shack out in the hill slums.

Years later, funded by the elderly gringo's charity, Rosa's husband Juan and some of the local residents set to work transporting water and local stone across the valley to a new settlement, Héroes del Cenepa. After weeks of hard labour, they completed two classrooms with a cardboard kitchen behind and a kerosene stove.

Rosa travelled into town to the Ministry of Education to register the fledgling school, but the official refused to accept such an inadequate construction. She smiled mischievously at me as she related how she wrung her hands and pleaded, and I imagined the male civil servant sitting opposite the young woman, her brown eyes shining with emotion, her wavy black hair falling around her high cheekbones, her delicate mouth, and her hands joined prayerfully as she begged for the sake of a few ragged kids in a desert slum.

He told her to send him photos of the rooms with desks covering the dirt floor and the shoddy walls hidden behind posters. She did as instructed, and against all odds, the creation of the primary school was duly approved.

'I promised him that we would improve things, little by little, as help came along. And over the years it did, and we managed what we could. There is much more to tell you, but for now, we have one hundred and thirty children, bursting out of the buildings, and a second storey with no roof!'

She stopped speaking, and in the cold, dank silence of the classroom, I studied the three anxious faces opposite me. Finally I nodded. 'I'll do what I can,' ... but the pledge in my heart went much further. I'd do everything in my power to support Rosa, her teachers, her school and its children, for as long as they needed me.

CHAPTER 10

I've come to check out the boyfriend and report back to the siblings,' announced Lisa as I flung my arms around her at Lima Airport. We flew back to Arequipa, where she stayed in my flat, dancing in the mornings with Emilio (who fell instantly in love with her), before setting out with me to the slums until midday, and passing the stormy afternoons at home with the cable TV while I taught classes in town.

February being the only month when nothing happened at Colegio Elohim, we caught the combi out to a squatter settlement in the foothills of Chachani, where I had volunteered with a small charity to teach a three-hour English class to local children every morning. Our stop to get off lay just beyond the last electricity pole, but on the first morning, with the volcano engulfed in cloud, we lost our bearings, and ended up wandering off course in the slum maze of shacks and laneways. Several fierce mongrels accosted us, but Lisa remained unfazed, thanks to her extraordinary connection with animals. 'Don't worry, Mum, he's smiling,' she assured me as she faced down a part-wolf, part-Alsatian baring its fangs, and I eventually stopped shaking as the enormous dog trotted off.

We finally arrived at a tiny tin-roofed cement classroom out in the middle of nowhere to find three other young volunteers, with forty local children eagerly awaiting us to sing and dance, complete word puzzles, and perform role-play in their first-ever English lesson.

'These kids are all picking up Australian accents!' said Lisa with a laugh as the unmistakable twang rang out from my 'Alphabet Rap' CD to be faithfully imitated by the whole class.

On the weekend Antonio passed muster when we went out for lunch, and one evening we met up with Nohémi, the two girls hitting it off right down to the tongue piercings. On Lisa's last day, we sipped tea together in the morning sun at a garden café and talked about friends at home, and that night, she headed off in the rain with her volunteer companions to the bus station to travel to Cusco.

I waved the taxi adios and turned away down the soggy street, feeling lost. She'd moved in, taken over my life for ten days, and now she'd gone, leaving a gaping, empty hole.

Thankfully it wouldn't be too long before we'd be together again, as I had plans to return to Australia two months later in April, to see Peter who'd be visiting from London. I contacted our local Sydney bowling club and booked it for a fundraiser for the second storey of Colegio Elohim.

In March, word came through that my work residency application had been approved, and I now had to travel to Arica, Chile, eighteen kilometres south of the Peruvian border, the closest place outside the country to collect the visa stamp. Meanwhile I could no longer leave Peru as a tourist … so with the planned trip to Sydney, the matter suddenly became urgent.

Five hours in a stuffy coach from Arequipa through the desert sun took me to the southern town of Tacna, the end of the road for Peruvian buses. There, head pounding from dehydration, I squashed with four other passengers into an ancient, rattling Chevy taxi to hurtle across a landscape of flat sand where even the prickly pear drooped and died. We crossed two border posts, one out of Peru and one into Chile, spied blue sea beyond the desolate coast, and eventually reached the drab outskirts of our destination.

I spent the following morning squeezed among fellow foreigners in the small waiting room of Arica's Peruvian Consulate-General until 1 pm, closing time, when an official emerged with a pile of passports. He handed them over, saying something which I didn't catch, but I heard the word 'Lima'.

'Perdón, Señor?'

He repeated more slowly, 'You have to take this visa, plus the required documentation, to Lima within twenty days to obtain your Carné Extranjería.'

I stared, my heart by now somewhere in the region of my stomach. Lima? Carné? A card?

In Arequipa, at 11 pm the same night, I emerged from the bus, temples still thumping, and fell into the arms of Antonio, blurting out my woes. 'Vamos!' he replied, eyes glinting with determination, and next morning's opening time at our local Immigration office found us sitting opposite a señorita who handed over a list of requirements. They leapt out from the blue page – several signed legal copies, three forms from a website, six photos, two sworn declarations, another four payments to the Banco de la Nación, and a dental impression.

'Help!' I swallowed a scream.

The next two hours flew past in a blur of taxis, bank queues, flash photography, and the dentist's chair, a simple check with a clean wooden spatula. As we cleared each hurdle, Antonio turned for a high five before charging off with me in tow to the next assignment. Twenty-four hours later, the list of requirements completed, we presented the lot to the same señorita. Somewhat astonished, she checked them over, tapped out a carbon-copied form on a typewriter, took imprints of every sticky finger on my left and right hands, plus both thumbs, and promised to send everything to Lima immediately.

In order to finally obtain the residency card, I now faced a return trip to the capital, to Inmigraciones and Interpol. All in Spanish, all alone, without Antonio's energy, protection, language and local knowledge. I had only four days before everything ground to a halt for the Easter break; a desperate deadline, for without the carné, I wouldn't be able to fly home to Australia, my son, and the fundraiser.

In Lima I struggled with a fog of instructions, dashed by taxi all over the city, made desperate international calls shouting into a smelly public phone amid the din and fumes of the evening rush hour; and transacted a midnight electronic payment to Australia plus several daylight deposits into local banks. Finally emerging from the Immigration building at 2 pm the day after I'd arrived, I clutched my passport and a small laminated plastic card. I checked my name, my photo, and the words *Carné Extranjería*. I'd got it, in time to catch my late afternoon plane back to Arequipa to resume my classes remaining before Easter … thanks, entirely, to the kindness of others, at every step.

I flew over the desert hills turned soft pink by the setting sun, my mind replaying the surreal events of the previous thirty-six hours. I recalled the desk of Inmigraciones, where I'd dissolved into tears in the face of rapid, incomprehensible Spanish as staff did their best to explain complicated processes to me, and how I'd finally ended up huddled on the front steps of Lima Interpol. A Costa Rican newlywed couple found me and shepherded me to the nearest internet café to find the location of the Australian Consulate-General, before putting me safely into a taxi, and giving the address to the driver. As I gasped my thanks and gripped their hands, the young man said simply, 'Today you needed angels, and God delivered us to you.'

At midnight just over forty-eight hours later, once again in Lima airport, I brandished my shiny new Peruvian residency card in the departures hall as I passed through Immigration; then headed for the gate to board my flight to Australia.

★

'Heads or tails!'

Back in Sydney, laughing guests stood clasping their skulls or their bottoms in one of the games which would cost them most of their small change. They had all rallied to the fundraiser, bringing along enough food for a multitude, cash and cheques. A booklet of stories and photos from my first eight months in Peru sold out in aid of the cause, together with weavings, pottery and soft alpaca garments I had brought back. Individuals and local businesses donated goods and services for a silent auction, and in all the evening raised over $7000, enough to complete the walls and roof of the second storey of Colegio Elohim.

The house was bursting with young people: Katy and her husband; Lisa, returned from her travels; Rachel, still studying; and Peter and his girlfriend, safely arrived from London. I felt ecstatic to be reunited with them all.

'You're blooming!' my friends exclaimed. 'You must be in love.'

I told them about my new romantic adventure and listened to their enthusiastic plans for us to live 'six months here and six months there'. I stayed silent about practicalities like acute economic inequality, Latin male pride, cultural differences and, frankly, how little I knew about Antonio; not to mention immigration, Australian and Peruvian.

'Lisa said he's okay.' Thus the siblings gave their approval. Meanwhile I began to feel my first pangs of anxiety about Katy's marriage, observing her working hard to support her husband's full-time studies, which didn't seem to leave much time for pleasure and relaxation.

A few days later, I stood in the queue for the cash register in the same old supermarket where I'd always shopped, only this time the trolley was filled not with small children buried by groceries, but packets of party pies and sausage rolls, and several bottles of tomato sauce for Rachel's nineteenth birthday party. It was a special celebration with her sisters and brother all present, and on the evening, back in the kitchen, sipping from the glass of dry Australian red, I felt myself ease into a twenty-year-old pattern as I pulled the tray of hot savoury pastries from the oven, taste-tested one, then handed them round.

'Thanks, Mum!' sputtered the young crowd as they lunged for more with mouths already full. Richard made an appearance, and even though we spoke only briefly and carefully, I could almost have thought that nothing had changed.

I went with Peter and his partner to the Blue

Mountains, where we walked in the bush down valleys and gorges, rock-hopped across creeks and under tumbling waterfalls, then enjoyed lunch in a restaurant with a spectacular view over sandstone cliffs. Too soon came the day I delivered them both to the airport and drove slowly away. Tears blurred my view in the rear-vision mirror of the young couple standing outside the terminal, his head bowed as she put her arms around him. Next came my turn as the one dropped off, once again swallowing sobs, for the return trip to Arequipa.

CHAPTER 11

When I caught the combi up to Colegio Elohim the day after I landed, I found men and women hoisting bags of cement, spadefuls of sand, and heavy buckets of water to pour into small concrete mixers, while their toddlers pottered and splashed in the puddles and dust nearby. The school had been transformed into a construction site, the funds raised in Sydney having already been transferred.

Less than a month later, came the day for the local tradition of the blessing of the new roof of the completed building. As I'd organised raising the money, I had to officiate. Balancing a huge supermarket bag full of sweets, I picked my way through the builders' rubble, up the rickety wooden ladder, and onto the just-completed, seismically-sound flat cement roof. Leaning over as far as I dared, I peered down into the dusty courtyard where dozens of eager young faces spotted me and started yelling, 'Caramelitos, Mees

Soosi!' Scooping out a handful, I flung them outwards, the squeals from below telling me they'd hit their mark.

Next came the cheap champagne at six soles a bottle, created especially for this purpose and definitely not for drinking. The head builder brought it over and wedged it carefully between two bricks, handing me a hammer. I held my breath and Whack! the glass collapsed in splinters and champagne froth oozed everywhere. Shouts floated up to me. 'Más caramelitos!' They wanted more, so I hurled dozens of treats in all directions, children scrambling to grab them, several flinging themselves into the dust to get ahead. A female yell rang out in the distance – a group of women, manual workers all in red municipality T-shirts, stumbled down the rocky hill opposite, calling out, laughing and waving their arms. I waited until they came closer, then threw their share into the dirt road outside the wall; impressed that they'd run so far for the chance to grab at a handful of sweets.

The new roof meant two more classrooms, their inside walls to be painted and plastered within the week. With enrolments steadily increasing, these couldn't come too soon to provide the space vital for the children.

Finally I shook the empty bag upside down to show my audience far below. 'See? None left!' The formalities completed, the roof had been blessed, bringing fair fortune to all those who gathered beneath it ... now

I just had to manoeuvre myself down the makeshift ladder, which seemed to be wobbling a lot more than it had on my way up.

By the middle of June, we had two ample, airy upstairs classrooms. 'Good morning, everyone,' I'd begin, surveying the children standing behind their new desks, bought with the remainder of the funds we had raised. 'Goot Mowni, Mees Soosi,' they chanted in reply. As I moved around, helping with paired conversations, Misti's rugged folds loomed just beyond the window; and Chachani, his mighty snow-dusted brother, brooded in the near distance. My pupils had some view if they got bored.

Around this time, Antonio took me to an agricultural show on the outskirts of town where I met llamas and alpacas with fluffy woollen coats and soft brown eyes, chewing their cud with buck teeth. I took my seat in the stadium and held my breath as two gigantic bulls, one brown and one black, locked horns and pushed at each other to cheers and flying cowboy hats, until eventually the black one prevailed and forced the other to retreat. Afterwards, Antonio posed for a photo, in straw hat, jeans and checked shirt, artistically draping a fence, unaware that at that same moment, right behind him, the massive brown bull was being hauled from the arena. Still furious and humiliated, hooves stamping, horns down, the poor creature snorted and strained to charge the provocative denim-blue backside on the wooden bars right in front of his nose; while four cattle herders, heaving on ropes, struggled to stay upright in the dust and restrain him. I froze behind the camera, not sure whether to laugh or scream, until the men prevailed and the danger passed.

As we were about to leave, Antonio stopped, listening. His face lit up as he cried, 'La marinera!', grabbed my hand and pulled me towards faint sounds of drumrolls and brass band music, which strengthened as we reached an arena, where several couples stood, poised. The young women, exquisitely made up, glossy hair pulled back by combs wound with flowers, wore colourful satin dresses with slim-fitting bodices and calf-length full skirts and petticoats. They smiled brightly, wrapped in the arms of handsome young men dressed in crisp white long-sleeved shirts with black satin vests, high-waisted tailored pants and shiny heeled boots; every one holding a wide-brimmed hat in his hand … which he raised as he leaned in to kiss his partner in a joyfully theatrical gesture. The dance continued as the bare-footed girls began to tap, stamp and prance, toes curling, swishing and swirling their gorgeous skirts around them with one hand, deftly holding aloft a fluttering white handkerchief with the other. The men mirrored their movements, torsos erect and barely seeming to move while their feet flew right and left, forward and back, balancing the straw hat in one hand as they leapt and bowed.

A loud honk came from beside me and I turned to see Antonio blowing his nose, tears streaming. 'It is the pride of our country, this dance,' he sobbed. When he had recovered himself enough he continued. 'The steps imitate the prance of our Paso horse, which does not trot or canter. It "ambles", left side to right side. Its legs seem to flick out sideways from its body. See? Just as the boys are doing.'

I saw it immediately, how the intricate dance mimicked the graceful animal, and a burst of Peruvian patriotism took me by surprise as it surged through me.

Not for anything did I miss my own opportunities to dance in the morning sessions at the club. Even in a tracksuit, Emilio managed to bring a sexiness to everything from cumbia to reggaetón. I kept my eyes firmly on him, and not myself in the mirror, as I blundered my way through the huaynos, stamping with hands behind my back while somehow shaking my bust at the same time; the saya, feet turning and hips twisting to the drum and pan pipes, vibrating right through me; the samba with its wild backward skip; salsa and merengue, trying to get a fluid motion on top while the toes stumbled around down below. Most exhausting of all, the festeja, the wildly rhythmic dance first done by African slaves brought to Peru by the Spanish. Hands up, bottom out, shoulders back and forth, knees bent, spine arched and stretched to breaking point, and all to the hypnotic beat of the hollow box drum. As it thumped through me, and various women shrieked in the sheer exhilaration of the dance, I wobbled everything till I thought I'd explode with joy and laughter. By the time Emilio invited me onto the platform to dance it with him, I'd thrown all caution to the wind; and I did okay, for a gringa.

Peruvian Father's Day arrived on the third Sunday in June. Antonio had organised a walk to the terraces, but shortly after his arrival, he went silent and continued to sulk all day. When I finally confronted him he announced he was upset because I hadn't given him a gift, which I found odd as he was father neither of me, nor of my children. I'd been surprised and touched by the attention he'd lavished on me for Mother's Day, but I had not realised the importance of the corresponding festival for fathers. I made some caustic comments about 'conditional love' which I regretted once I'd cooled down.

Three days later he came to me and asked for forgiveness. I gratefully accepted his apology and we moved on … but it did occur to me how Richard must have felt when I'd held out on my own angry huffs, and why he'd seemed less than understanding of my tearful attempts to atone.

Antonio organised tickets to a concert by an artist from Lima, in his sixties and famed for his innovative traditional Andean music using original instruments. Peru, and particularly Arequipa, has a proud tradition of musical and literary talent, and a renowned intelligentsia. Authors such as Mario Vargos Llosa and Alfredo Bryce Echeneque, living abroad, and musicians like the young Lucho Quequezana, back in Lima after successes overseas.

The performance was billed to begin at 8 pm under the stars in the elegant stone cloisters of the Iglesia de la Compañía on a corner of the Plaza de Armas. We arrived at 7.40 pm and took our place at the end of a long queue down two blocks and around the corner from the cloisters' entrance, firmly shut, with three monstrous padlocks holding the security grille. We stood waiting, along with our fellow citizens, in their formal best suits, dresses and shiny shoes, huddled in overcoats and shivering against the sharp chill of the desert night. Sellers in tracksuits and worn coats patrolled with trays of sweets and chocolates, deep fried snacks, or even offering places at the head of the queue which they had come especially to secure hours earlier in the hope of selling them on at a profit.

On the dot of 8 pm, two uniformed security guards appeared, each with an impressive bunch of keys, and after some unhurried fiddling, inserted the three largest into the locks, and heaved the gates open. They positioned themselves on either side to check the tickets, complete with revolvers and batons just in case we docile and elderly music-lovers decided to riot. We eventually found our places and sat down expectantly at 8.15 pm.

At 9 pm we were still there, nothing having happened except a few fleeting appearances of busy musicians and technicians fine-tuning enormous black sound boxes, and the star himself, wandering across the stage glancing in surprise at us as if he'd forgotten why three hundred-odd people might be sitting around waiting for something. By the time the band finally struck up, my mood had plummeted from excited to plain grumpy; in my freezing seat, numb bottom, yawning from cold, boredom and tiredness. If he played with talent, I didn't notice.

I harangued Antonio during the interval with a comparison to a night at the Sydney Opera House where you can enjoy a drink in the – open – foyer and when ready, make your way to the theatre door where a gentleman or lady in dinner suit greets you, checks your ticket and courteously shows you to your seat. And if you arrive late – no matter if you happen to be the Prime Minister or even the Queen – the same courteous lady or gentleman in dinner suit will politely show you where you can wait outside, until a suitable break in the performance, which commenced when it was supposed to, at the advertised hour.

Antonio told me that the distinguished members of Arequipeñan society made a point of delaying their grand entrance, and everybody, audience and performers alike, waited for them, thus reinforcing their sense of importance. Naturally, when people know things won't start on time, they all arrive late. I huffed and puffed with indignation. 'So they see it as a matter of pride to keep everybody waiting? It's just plain bloody rude! A week of punctuality and locking the doors to stragglers would fix it.'

'Aye, Soosita,' sighed Antonio, 'only mass begins on time in this country. Oh, and classes at the institute.'

Visiting the ladies', I found a fancy facility, but no soap in the holders, and toilets all missing seats.

'In case people remove them,' whispered Antonio as the band tuned up again. I hunkered down into my uncomfortable chair, arms folded. Did they think you'd stuff the toilet seat up under your dinner jacket before or after the performance? So that was why the super-sized rolls of loo paper always hung outside, not inside, the cubicles … to prevent people secretly stealing it. What a trap for the unwary who realised, sitting bare-bottomed on the toilet (with no seat), that the vital accessory was on the other side of the locked door!

I signed up to perform in Emilio's group for the Danzathón, a bi-annual event at the club which always created mayhem. The normal timetable was overturned to give way to feverish preparations as every instructor worked with a selection of dancers to finally lead them in a special number before an exuberant audience. After two weeks of rehearsals cancelled because no-one, least of all Emilio, turned up on time (except me), our team somehow managed to master the routine with mere moments to spare.

On the appointed costume-buying day, everyone finally arrived at the market, and we set off into the labyrinth of stalls, past blaring TVs and CDs, and shouting vendors and selling a vast array of pirated products in a fug which smelt of the meat stews bubbling in the lunch canteens.

After losing everyone at least once, several intense

discussions and trying on multiple garments in dark corners behind pulled curtains, we finally reached agreement on a T-shirt; then headed for the wigs. Giggling like schoolgirls, we selected an assortment of styles and colours from platinum blonde to orange and purple, Emilio choosing a black frizz number with dark plastic glasses for further effect.

On the day of the Danzathón, I quivered with a nervous dread of forgetting the steps and going blank. Finally the moment came, and the theme song from *Rocky* belted out, our cue to enter … cloaked in black, hooded capes, throwing them off to reveal our ridiculous outfits to shrieks and roars from the crowd. Then we shimmied and shook, rocked 'n rolled our way through our routine, finally prancing off-stage waving our arms singing, 'We'll aaalways be togeeether!' The crowd went mad, clapping, shouting and throwing things in the air, a fitting tribute to our memorable performance … and utterly unforgettable hairstyles.

CHAPTER 12

Afew weeks later, Antonio and I were invited to the wedding of two young work colleagues at the pretty Spanish colonial church on the Plaza Yanahuara, just near my flat. Arriving early beneath a clear sky on Saturday for the noon start, we strolled around the plaza, past the ragged sweet-seller rattling her chewing gum packets at cheerful tourists as they enthused in a range of languages at the view over Arequipa's snow-tipped volcanoes. Seven different bridal couples had assembled in various spots to pose for photo shoots – balanced in a kiss on the carefully swept steps of the municipal hall, relaxing on the wall of the fountain with fingers fluttering in the water, gazing at bright flowerbeds, and seated on areas of mown grass beneath the palm trees amid circular skirts and petticoats. Every pair strategically separated from the others, they recorded memories of their special day in this chic location, popular with the aspiring middle class. Their be-ribboned, gleaming cars awaited them, magenta Chevrolets and vintage black Mercedes decked out with flowers, slotted in between tourist buses on the only street where parking was permitted. We paused to admire smiling young women in various creations of white silk and taffeta, their attendants wearing matching outfits in hues from pastel to strident, setting off strikingly made-up eyes and elaborately styled dark hair, on the arms of proud men in impeccable formal suits and ties.

On our way back to the entrance of the church, we greeted other guests before moving with them beneath the carved portal to the interior, cool and shadowy but not at all gloomy thanks to the white stone cupola roof. I took my seat next to Antonio on a polished wooden pew and glanced sideways at the effigy of Jesus in His glass coffin, at rest until the next Good Friday when He would be carried out and around the plaza in procession. At the front of the nave rose the wooden cross, with Him suffering horribly upon it, watched by a statue of His mother, and two minor saints, all of whom would also be hoisted onto faithful shoulders to perambulate amid prayers and lighted candles at the appropriate times on the Catholic religious calendar.

Today, however, was a more joyful occasion, and as the organ struck up, we all turned to see a veiled vision standing in the entrance, backlit by the bright Arequipa sunshine, ready to make her way down the aisle to a new phase in her life. She began her journey, slow and smiling, and I'm sure many minds in the lovely chapel travelled back to their own ceremonies; but mine, unwilling to linger, chose to retreat further in time, to a glamorous post-war wedding which never took place.

Ten years after Dad died, Mum followed him, and on the order of service for her funeral we printed the story she'd written for us of the bridal dress she never wore.

'I was to marry my English naval commander in July 1946, and all was planned and ready for the Sydney society event; but then my beloved father died suddenly just a week before the intended date. Everything had to be severely scaled down, with cancellation notices sent out to all the guests, and in the end I married in a plain day dress at a simple ceremony with just my groom, watched by my poor grieving mother and a few close friends.

'So what to do with my wedding gown? It had been sewn out of parachute silk which Dad had somehow acquired in Singapore, and it was far too precious to leave behind. So it travelled with me on an ocean liner in my luggage to the top floor of a draughty stone house in Scotland, my first home as a naval wife. I soon made some friends, among them a young girl who wanted to marry, but couldn't find any material to make her dress because of the severe post-war rationing. So in the end, my gorgeous garment proceeded down the aisle adorning a local lassie while I stood watching in the congregation!'

More than fifty years later, her friends told me that as they sat quietly reading the story before her funeral began in St James' Anglican Church on Sydney's North Shore, they heard her, laughing lightly as she told it; as if they were all together at just another card gathering over afternoon tea.

'En el Nombre del Padre, del Hijo, y del Espiritu Santo, Amen.' Here on the other side of the world, in San Juan Bautista Catholic Chapel in Arequipa's Plaza Yanahuara, the entire congregation performed the genuflexion, and the service was over. We stood as the radiant couple strode joyfully out of the church to the waiting vehicle and took off towards their life together; beginning with the reception. All we guests hailed small taxis which materialised instantly to take us along to celebrate with the newlyweds.

The bride's parents lived in a substantial home in the suburbs with a garden where a marquee had been set up with decorated tables and chairs, a dance floor and a band. We took our places at a table with eight other people, only two of whom we knew. My castellano had improved enough to allow some conversation with the new acquaintances, much of it responding to inquiries about my children, what I was doing here, my relationship with Antonio, how much it cost to fly to Australia … I now knew how to field such prying questions from people who didn't know me, realising they were not meant to offend, but were rather due to curiosity about my different appearance. It was all just proof, though more benign, of Antonio's comment after my street assault that someone would always be watching me.

He conversed easily and seemed at ease and proud to have me with him. As the afternoon progressed into evening, the waiters brought round food and offered plenty of pisco, but after two sours, I stuck with water. When the band struck up and Antonio asked me to dance, I felt my body relax and my feet follow his lead, as he held me firmly in the small of my back and guided me through the steps of the Peruvian waltzes he'd danced since he could stand.

By 11.30 pm, we had been there for nine and a half hours, everyone had clearly indulged in a good deal of alcohol, and I was exhausted, ready to go home. At midnight, the waiters brought out bottles of whiskey and placed two at each table, to the obvious delight of all. *You're kidding*. I watched shots poured and downed, and refused one urged on me.

'We Peruvians love our whiskey,' Antonio said as he drained his glass in one gulp and refilled it.

We left about half an hour later. As we emerged from the warmth of the party to the cold, deserted street, Antonio became increasingly confused about which direction we should take. After a few moments of talking to him I realised he was making no sense.

Too embarrassed to return to the marquee, I tried to get my bearings, helped him up a dark flight of steps, and heaved a sigh of relief as I recognised the main road into town. I hailed the first taxi which came into view, got Antonio home to my flat and put him to bed. I crawled in beside him to lie awake and frightened in a haze of pisco and whiskey fumes as he mumbled and ground his teeth all night. Alcohol was clearly a significant part of Peruvian culture, but hadn't this gone a bit too far?

The next morning Antonio was mortified when I revealed what had occurred. He remembered nothing after he'd left the reception. 'I'm so sorry. This has never happened to me before.'

But then I figured, if you lived alone, with nobody to tell you, how would you know?

As my grasp of castellano improved, I began to understand what went on in the lives of the slum children of Colegio Elohim; the abuse so many endured behind closed doors inside their dingy shacks; and their heart-breaking resilience as they turned up for school each day.

Veronica, in Grade 6 English, often came to school in dusty street clothes, thick black hair matted and face dirty, smelling none-too-sweet. Some mornings she simply laid her head on the desk and closed her eyes, but on others, her English conversations and answers revealed a sharp mind. I asked Yulissa, her teacher, about her background and heard for the first time about her mother, Pamela. This swarthy, stout woman had four children at the time and one on the way. Veronica was the oldest, followed by Lucía, Sofía and Marcelo.

'Ah, Veronica,' sighed Yulissa. 'She started at Elohim aged just five, a dishevelled little mite she was, often so hungry she'd fall asleep on the floor. She struggled on – with nothing. Never had a book or even a pencil, but we did what we could to help her along. She told me once about scrabbling in the rubbish tips down in that horrible part where she lives, to find newspapers or magazines to practise reading. And now see how far she's come. She's made it through primary school to Grade 6. Gracias a Dios.'

I visited Pamela's hovel some time later when the school was closed for holidays, and saw, and smelt, the life they endured. Skirting round several chickens and dogs grubbing outside in the dust, we stooped to enter a dim room which stank of old cooking fat and urine. I made out a bed with a tattered mattress where a small child lay asleep – Pamela's latest addition, Rafael, almost two.

'Let's dance!' cried Marcelo. The naked electrical outlet in the wall sparked blue in the gloom as he plugged in a battered machine and inserted a pirated

CD. I stumbled over a kerosene cooker by the door to join him, and as we bobbed around on the dirt floor, I spotted a small television on a shelf in one corner, half-obscured by a pile of rags. Rosa had told me that Pamela had bought it some years before, with money donated by a well-meaning gringo, shocked at the state of Veronica and her siblings. As I joined arms with Marcelo for a twirl, I thought about the lure of escapism.

We stepped out again into the yard. Devoid of sanitation, it nonetheless boasted a cold water tap – a luxury which hadn't yet reached us further up the hill at Colegio Elohim – and a tin basin of clothes waited, soaking, to be hung out to dry. We gave Pamela five soles so Marcelo could run to the store to buy milk for the family, the first nourishment they'd had all day.

Pamela's husband had abandoned them years before, but returned at intervals to exercise his conjugal rights in the bed in the one room shared by the whole family, every visit resulting in another pregnancy. Staring round me, I wondered how Pamela dragged herself up each morning to face a new day.

I suspected Veronica's intelligence, and that equally evident in Sofía and Marcelo, came from their mother who, while never having learned to read or write, behaved with a canny street cunning. But neither Veronica's intellect, nor the love and encouragement of her years at Colegio Elohim, would save her from the pitfalls facing vulnerable girls caught up in the grinding poverty of the macho slums of Arequipa.

★

When the institute entered a regional dance competition, Antonio and I joined the cheer squad, to support our contestants. I was familiar with the saya they would be performing, having already encountered it with Emilio … in tracksuit and lycra; but our two young colleagues arrived at the venue for the performance wearing long-sleeved, open-collared waisted jackets with stiff, shiny panels of black, yellow and red. Below, the girl's tiny matching skirt barely covered her bottom, revealing her long, shapely stockinged legs all the way down to her high heels. The boy's jodhpur-style pants featured a row of silver bells adorning each snug-fitting calf, and black leather-heeled cowboy boots.

When the twelve competing couples began, the womens' skirts swirled horizontally over their rotating hips, revealing petticoats and knickers as their feet skipped and arms and busts swayed. Beneath firmly fastened little hats, long artificial plaits attached to their hair swung, bouncing the pompoms at their ends. The men's movements were an unambiguous display of virility, from their fist-clenching stamps to their high leaps and athletic knee-drops, heightened by the jangling of their bells. I grinned to myself as I imagined a bunch of Aussie blokes even attempting such a thing.

But as I watched and heard the cries of 'Eso! That's it! Eso!' from the excited audience, darker thoughts arose … of Pamela and her children, particularly her daughters, and of the life they could expect at the hands of the men of the slum society. Was this just a perverse extrapolation of the message of female coquettishness and male dominance now being played out before me? I began to realise how this dance that I so loved reflected the confusing, double-edged culture of this land.

CHAPTER 13

I had used up my annual month of holidays on my visit to Sydney, so to take more, I had to resign from the institute, although I knew I could always return in the future. Antonio and I travelled twelve hours by overnight bus from Arequipa to Cotahuasi Canyon, burrowed in our seats under our jackets, sipping from our smuggled cask of red wine. Even if he could have afforded a private car, driving it twelve hours through the deserted roads of the mountains would have been out of the question at any time of day or night, given the danger of hijacking and highway robbery.

We spent five days in a small hotel, taking local combis to traditional Andean villages dotted along the river beneath sheer cliffs, amid a patchwork of terraced fields, irrigated by a system of canals and streams built by the Incas. In a bathhouse we soaked in natural bubbling hot springs, overlooking the river rapids, and ate fresh trout from the small adjoining restaurant. Then again, perhaps not-so-fresh, because the morning after the meal I woke up with a telltale gurgling in my stomach, rushed to the toilet, and spent the next seventy-two hours in bed with food poisoning.

By the last morning I had recovered enough to walk with Antonio, slowly, to a waterfall tumbling to the canyon floor far below, and when we returned to the village I felt ready for a menú (without trout) for lunch at a table for two in a flower-filled garden. We set off at four in the afternoon in the public bus with all the locals, bound once again for Arequipa, driving up through hills patterned with fields of potatoes, beans, maize, and the pinky-yellow crops of quinua and kiwicha, luminous in the late afternoon sun. Once out of the canyon, I rested my head on his shoulder as we watched a spectacular sunset over the stark mountains.

Night came, and we all fell asleep, leaving the driver to negotiate the tortuous curves, rises and descents of the lonely road. Over the ensuing hours, we woke up twice for comfort stops – unforgettable spectacles, when the entire bus piled out in the middle of the desert, men at the front and ladies at the back – a display of brilliant stars in the black sky above, and white bared bottoms of every shape and size below, goose bumped in the frigid night air. Heaving up pants, zipping flies, we clambered back into the dense warmth of the bus and, lulled back to

sleep in our cramped seats by the bumping and swaying, soon resumed our snoring.

★

'Arequipa!' came the deep voice crackling over the
speaker as the bus slowed to a stop in pitch darkness
at the terminal. The sickly yellow lights came on
and I fumbled for my glasses to peer at my watch,
reading 3.30 am. Everyone stirred, gradually standing
up and stretching. Men hauled bundles in coloured
blankets from the luggage compartments, while
women gathered up slumbering infants in their strong
arms. I stumbled to the door and down the steps, still
half-asleep, the only gringa among the indigenous
passengers. Antonio also stood out as a tourist; tall,
slender, fairer-skinned, his thick, curly hair showing
his Spanish and African heritage.

We waited in the scrum when the luggage com-
partment opened, and Antonio finally grabbed our
bags and marched towards the terminal, where a small
crowd had gathered shouting, 'Taxi, taxi, Señor!' He
spoke rapidly to a young man in collared shirt and trousers, took off behind him and, still dazed, I obediently
followed. Passing a small white taxi in the carpark, its
driver sitting with his identification ticket clearly showing, I said, 'What about … ?' but neither loudly nor
persistently enough. We followed the chosen taxista

outside the terminal to a yellow tico parked in the street, Antonio helping me in while the driver put our luggage in the boot. The back window would not close, so now, I felt not only sleepy, but also bad-tempered and cold. At least we'd be home in a few minutes.

We turned into Cruz Verde, an old, dark, narrow street not much wider than a car, lined with high stone walls on each side. All of a sudden, a bright light shone into the back seat. I turned, squinting, and made out two spots on high beam bearing down on us, from what appeared to be a black jeep. I felt our taxi grinding to a halt, and made out five dark figures rushing forward into the brilliant light. Just as I realised they were wearing black balaclavas, one reached the door beside me and wrenched it open. A thought flashed through my mind. *If I crouch my feet up, I could give him a hefty shove in the chest.* But the chance evaporated as he launched himself on top of me, pushing a smelly rough rug over my face. I felt Antonio leaning over, hitting out and slapping at my assailant – until a deep growl came from his side, 'Viejo.' Old man. 'Cuchillo.' Knife.

Suddenly the struggling stopped and I realised Antonio, too, was underneath a blanket, another man, armed, holding him down and, from the voices, at least two more in front with the driver. Blinded, gasping, I felt the car begin to move again ... Antonio? I felt for his hand and it gripped mine. I clung on tight, counting and concentrating as I tried to find enough air to force into and out of my lungs. Soon my mind began to race. *Taxi abduction. They beat up their victims ... Laura from the institute hailed a cab downtown in broad daylight and woke up in hospital ... My passport and cards. In a money belt around my waist ... and this car dragging us away from any hope of rescue.*

A man ordered 'go faster' and, I guessed by the disgusted tone, added something about a 'rust bucket'. After about twenty minutes, it stopped, and I heard the doors being flung open. Someone hauled me outside. Still hooded, I stumbled and tripped over stones and into soft dust as he pushed me along, murmuring to his companions. I stepped onto cement and heard a metal door slam behind us. We'd ended up in some sort of garage or shed. Rough hands grabbed my head, yanking coarse bands round my eyes so tight I saw stars, then shoving me hard with a sharp command. 'Lie down,' murmured Antonio. I felt concrete, cold, damp under my back. I lay frozen, clinging to his arm, hearing zips opened, the contents of our backpacks cluttering out onto the ground. Our captors muttered as they fingered our things, taking their time and helping themselves.

About ten minutes later they'd gone quiet, and Antonio's hand squeezed mine, trembling ... he cleared his throat, speaking up in a strong, calm voice, 'I'm Peruvian. We're grandparents. We'll do everything you ask, just don't hurt us, we beg you, and let us go, so we can go back to our children and our grandchildren.' A barked reply came back, vile slang by its tone which I didn't understand, but Antonio did, and shuddered against me.

I tried to not to panic as I laboured to breathe, the thick covers pushing against my mouth and nose. Moments later, I felt them thrown off me, and a man speaking into my ear. Antonio whispered in English, 'If you don't hand over your valuables, they'll strip search you. Best do as they say.' I started to cry as I fumbled for my money belt, unable to control my shaking enough to undo the clip. Waiting fingers tapped sharply at my arm, until I finally got it off and handed it over. 'Número PIN,' demanded a rough voice. Somehow I remembered it, and stammered, 'uno, tres, cinco, dos'. Antonio repeated slowly and clearly, just to make sure, knowing that they'd go into town to find an automatic teller. If the numbers didn't work they'd come back.

The metal door opened and slammed again. A car revved out and away. Silence. Had they left us alone? I didn't dare move, or try to speak to Antonio in case they were still there, watching us. Then we heard men mumbling. I could make out just two ... until they were joined by a third speaker, much softer. A tremor surged through Antonio's body ... He'd heard it, and so had I ... a woman's voice.

Something I'd seen on the television news flashed into my mind. A dusty slum street glaringly lit by media cameras as police converged on a squalid shack, a furious mother racing out screaming, grabbing, hitting and punching as they dragged away her son in hooded tracksuit from where she'd been hiding him. I wondered if we'd ended up in such a place with such a woman. Thank heavens we were blindfolded.

The initial shock of our abduction eased, half the gang having gone into town and left us as kidnap hostages with our now silent minders. My body stopped shaking and passed into a sort of deathly, desperate boredom. Minutes later my bladder began to fill. I managed to ignore it for about half an hour, until the pressure got desperate. *Hell, what now?* I took a deep breath and called out into the nothingness beyond my bandaged eyes, 'Necesito orinar.' Immediately I felt someone near me – they can't have been far away at all – who began to haul me up under my arms, growling, 'Vamos al baño.'

'No!' I screamed. Not for anything would I let go of Antonio and stumble with this thug to an unknown toilet somewhere. 'Un bol, un bol.'

'Please, bring her a bowl,' translated Antonio, continuing firmly as I felt cold metal thrust into my hands, 'Now, give her some privacy.' Who knows if they watched or not as we pulled blindly to get my pants down, so I could squat, and aim into the bowl. I finally finished and raised my bare bottom so they could take it out without slopping its warm contents, then scrambled to somehow pull up my dignity while still crouching. One of our minders said, 'Stay quiet, Mamita, and you'll get out of this unharmed.' Sweetie? Was that supposed to reassure me? He offered us water but we both refused; opting for dehydration over another 'bowl' procedure.

Someone switched on a radio, with reggaetón and salsa, an eerie reminder of the normal, free world we'd been wrenched from. Time signals gave clues as the morning dragged on. I listened to the music, forcing myself to remember Emilio's dance steps, and make up new ones. Mobile phones rang every so often; and I caught fragments ... 'Wow! Fuck yeah! Good one!' ... and presumed the thugs in the city were ringing to say how much money they'd got out on our cards. Later I heard, 'No, mi amorcito, I'm not out drinking and I'm not in trouble.'

'Ritmo felicidad. Las dos de la tarde.' The radio, tuned to 'Happiness Rhythm', announced 2 pm. Ten hours had crawled past and sweat soaked through my clothes as the afternoon sun bore down onto what I guessed would be a plastic calamine roof above us. I whimpered that I was hot, and my guard came over and pulled back my blanket, adjusting my blindfold. Slightly more comfortable now, ignoring my dead numb behind, I tried to meditate, to conjure up light beings, buddhas, angels, even hummingbirds around me, anything I could think of to ward off the hysteria.

Footsteps rushed in, and someone flicked the radio up to full volume. I felt my feet grabbed, and rope being tied savagely around my ankles. Then my wrists were forced together in front of me as someone wound the cord around them. All morning I had been praying they would not realise that if they kept me prisoner, they could take out my daily limit from my debit card every twenty-four hours for weeks, months … Had they worked it out? Was I to be taken and left to rot in some shed in the pitiless sun, never to be found, while they lived off my savings? The urgency of my attacker's movements suggested that he was angry.

Then, just as suddenly as he'd stormed in, he stormed out again, leaving me stunned, the radio still blaring. Perhaps they'd all run away, frightened off by something, maybe the police. I squeezed Antonio's hand, and felt its response. He was obviously wondering the same. *Can I get these ropes off? Could we make a break for it?*

A commotion of footsteps and voices came through the door. The brief flash of hope gave way to another detonation of intense fright. He's still here! But the footsteps hurried over, turned down the music and untied me. I realised our guards must have returned to watch over us again. I couldn't believe it. I had no clue what had just happened, but my mind still squirmed with horrifying images of what could have. Relieved of my bonds, I lay shaking out of control. Our 'minders' spoke softly some distance away, but I strained to listen and heard the concern in their voices and snippets about how long we two elderly people had been held captive. The individual who'd just burst in, however, was nothing short of a maniac, and now my whole body tensed every time I heard any movement.

Our kidneys ached with chill as the afternoon sun crept away and we heard 5 pm on the radio. Another three hours gone. At one point I moaned loudly and slumped forward in the hope that if I fainted, they'd let us go, to get rid of me quicker. Antonio threw in some inspired nonsense about my congenital heart condition. Our guards conferred and made a call but after a grumbled, 'Yeah boss, okay … okay already!' they stayed put, mute and unmoved.

The cheerful DJ announced 6 pm. We'd been lying there for twelve hours, blindfolded, too terrified to speak, let alone move. As the evening cold seeped up from the cement floor, darkness filtered through our blindfolds. We clutched each other tighter, daring to hope that they would soon deem it late enough to dump us somewhere without attracting attention. If they left us out in the desert, how would we survive the night? My heart started thumping. The 8 pm jingle sounded on the radio.

Suddenly, a mobile phone rang, and after a whispered conversation, our minders pulled us to our feet. One led me around in circles, growling, 'Come on. If you faint in the car we'll keep you here till mornin'. Pull yourself together.' I felt sick as I realised that my ruse had backfired and may lead to another night's captivity. I walked strongly and steadily to convince him of my miraculous recovery. The maniac hadn't returned … I no longer even cared about the icy desert night so long as they let us go.

The man yanked my beanie over my head above the blindfold. 'We've gotta cover ya' hair so no-one sees.' We heard a car approach, stop with the engine idling, and at least four men burst in, grabbing us and hustling us outside. Shivering and stumbling, we fell into the back of a car, doubtless the same taxi we'd arrived in. Antonio risked saying to me softly in English, 'I think this ordeal may be coming to an end.'

They all squashed in and drove us round this way and that, blackness and bright street lights flashing like a strobe through our blindfolds. We clung to each other as they sniggered. Then one even began chatting to

Antonio, whose body shook as he somehow managed to respond in kind, even laughing when his cowardly tormentor joked, 'We'll give you fifty soles for a taxi home – but be fuckin' careful which one you get.'

'And by the way, old man,' he added, 'don't get any ideas about goin' to the police, 'cos we got friends and we'll know. We got your address from your DNI and we'll be round to visit.'

Antonio shuddered. I knew his identity card bore the address of the family home, where his ex-wife and daughter still lived. This crime would go unreported.

Finally, after about thirty minutes, someone grabbed my hand and shoved something into it. My passport. I slipped my finger inside it and felt the reassuring plastic of what I prayed was my Carné Extranjería. Moments later, my backpack was dumped in my lap. 'We're gonna stop, take off your blindfolds, and let you out. Face away from the car, stand still, hold your bags in front of your chests and count to forty. Don't dare turn around – you do, and we see you, we'll be back.' We nodded – death in any form suddenly seemed infinitely preferable to being picked up again by this bunch. The car stopped, they ripped the bands from our eyes, shoved us out of the car, and disappeared in a cloud of dust. We both scrambled upright and stood like statues, our eyes adjusting, for at least sixty seconds; then Antonio dropped his pack, unzipped his fly, groaned, and peed.

Above us, a sealed surface glowed beneath street lamps, leading to a small shop; they'd dumped us in one of the far outer desert suburbs. I peered at my watch, still on my wrist, thanks to my pleading in pidgin Spanish that it was not a Rolex, not valuable, a gift from my long-deceased parents … and they'd let it go. It was 9.15. We had been in the hands of this gang for over seventeen hours.

Antonio put his arm around me and I buried my face in his jacket. We hoisted our depleted backpacks and made our way slowly up the dusty slope toward the lights. Mongrels ran out at us, howling and barking, and I kicked out at one, letting out all the helpless terror of the day in a screaming tirade of broad Australian curses, until the creature retreated, tail between its legs.

We crept into the shop and told our story to the lady behind the counter. In no time several others had come in and offered us bananas, juice and advice. They helped us call a secure taxi, and we sat, trembling, in the back while the driver kept up a comforting conversation all the way home. We paid him with the fifty soles our kidnappers had given us. But at least our ID documents had been returned to us intact.

When we finally opened the door to my flat around 10.30 pm and dropped our packs, we clung together and wept. We spent hours on the phone and internet, cancelling cards and finding out the damage. They'd withdrawn $3000 cash before the machine had swallowed my cards, and cleaned out Antonio's holiday pay from his, deposited the day before.

All that, at last, done, I cooked a cheese omelette. We relished every mouthful, followed by a hot shower, toothpaste and toothbrush, and my warm, safe bed. Skin clean and fragrant, mouths tingling sweet and fresh, breathing gratefulness, relief and freedom, we finally fell asleep.

CHAPTER 14

Antonio rang his son and daughter the following day, and within twelve hours had told the tale and wept with his five siblings, ex-wife, and many work colleagues and friends. Nohémi appeared on the doorstep and hugged her father fiercely. 'Now, Papá,' she said, tears belying her stern tone, 'here's my mobile phone number. You are to call me every four hours.'

I returned to dance class, saying nothing about the ordeal. As I swayed to the same songs I'd heard during those hours beneath that blanket, relief flooded through me, bringing tears which I'm sure puzzled Emilio and my companions. How could I have explained? I was free once again; to dance, to sing, to laugh, to cry, to choose. To live.

Several days later, I sent word to my children, knowing there was little they could do, despite the pleas which came back for me to leave Peru at once. For the moment I couldn't bring myself to tell anyone else.

We tried to move on with our lives, and a few days later we had to take a taxi to transport some heavy boxes. It ran out of petrol in a busy street in the heart of Arequipa in broad daylight. As soon as the car slowed, I tensed, and as it ground to a halt, I leapt out and ran over to a guard at the bank across the road, grabbing hold of his arm. He smiled valiantly, thinking the gringa tourist wanted a photo. I clung on tightly and didn't let go until he finally understood, and put us both safely into a substitute vehicle.

Ten days after the kidnapping, a group of trekkers, three gringos and one extremely excited Peruvian, set off for the four-day Santa Cruz circuit in the Cordillera Blanca, my birthday present to Antonio. Luckily we both had enough funds to manage in separate Peruvian accounts which had escaped the robbery, so we had caught the overnight bus north from Lima to Caraz, determined to continue with a reduced version of the holiday we'd planned. Together with a Canadian couple, both experienced walkers, a local guide and two porters, we headed out of the town, but not before Antonio had rushed at the last moment to the market, and come back with a teal-green hand towel bearing a bright yellow Tweetie bird with a caption 'I tawt I taw …' Hooked across the back of his pack every day to dry, it resembled a giant canary hopping from bush to rock and meant that we never once lost him.

We picked our way up a steep path in sunshine beside a tumbling stream, alpine peaks coming into view all around us as we ventured higher. 'Aye, Soosita,' he enthused, 'it is all so glorious. My countrymen have little idea of the wonders we have on our doorstep. Such beauty ... and fresh air. They do not know what they are missing.'

At camp on our first night, after sausages and chips for dinner, we stood in wonder beneath a black sky incandescent with stars. 'Ah, La Cruz del Sur,' murmured Antonio.

'We call it the Southern Cross,' I said, taking his hand as we gazed up at the brilliant pointers whose benevolent guidance had been equally fundamental to us both, growing up on opposite shores of the Pacific.

We finally dragged ourselves away to our tent. As we lay side by side in our sleeping bags, I was just drifting off when a piercing light suddenly shone in my eyes and I woke with a start to hear Antonio gasping, 'I can't see!' He'd pulled his head torch on sideways so, while he blinded me, he couldn't see a thing in front of him. Stifling giggles, I reached up and adjusted it. Crouched awkwardly, he pulled on his boots and jacket, grabbed the toilet paper, eventually ripped the tent zip open, and bolted out into the cold darkness for the latrine.

We posed in a hug for a photo at the highest point of the trek, the rocky, snow-covered Punta Unión Pass at 4760 metres, which Antonio managed easily. Small children came to our camps to sell soft drinks and beer. When our companions expressed doubts about purchasing alcohol from a nine year old, he suggested, 'Amigos, anything you buy will help them and their families. At least they have some pride and do not beg.' He'd always ask the youngsters for a can or two of beer, and question them earnestly, 'Little daughter, have you been to school today? Where do you go? What class are you in? Listen, if you don't want to spend your life selling drinks to rich tourists, you must get an education. It is the most important thing of all. It will give you choice and make you free. Understand?' They nodded slowly, staring at him with round eyes.

At our last camp, I watched him in the late afternoon sunshine by a clear flowing stream, rinsing his socks, humming to himself. He suddenly dropped them on the grass and began clapping a bolero rhythm, swaying his shoulders and singing in his clear, mellow voice, his face lit with a wide smile. He described our trek later as the four most wonderful days of his life.

The walk over, we spent a night of luxury in Lima in the deep bubble bath and huge twin beds of one of the city's oldest hotels. The next day, Antonio caught the bus back to Arequipa, while I flew out to the US and spent September visiting friends – New York, Toronto, Quebec, Las Vegas and San Francisco – a complete change of surroundings, and not one tiny yellow taxi in sight. During the trip I gradually divulged what had happened, and finally sent a message to my wider circle of family and friends, triggering an inundation of healing responses, including one from Richard. My Sydney meditation leader emailed helpful advice; to try to focus upon any mercy shown me during the ordeal. There had been plenty – our minders did the best they could to reassure us and keep us comfortable, nobody beat us up, they didn't steal our identities and they eventually let us go. I elected to see the abduction as a timely warning which, perhaps, saved us, and others, from something far worse. Indeed, my email was widely circulated by anxious parents to any members of the younger generation heading for South America.

I returned to Arequipa and initiated more radical changes. I avoided taking taxis alone, preferring to walk or catch the combi, and from then on, wherever possible, stopped going out at night. Any invitation produced instant anxiety as no party, wedding, dance or theatre event could justify the risk of ever getting into such a situation again. The worry about the ride home made it simply not worth the anguish, and Antonio felt the same. I felt danger lurking everywhere, particularly for a gringa who stood out from the crowd … even if she carried only a plastic bag and wore an oversized bra. My cards and documents stayed at home, and in my pockets I kept only small change.

Even the mayor of Yanahuara got into the wrong taxi one afternoon and his wife, my age, ended up badly bashed in the face. Alarmed press accounts summed up Peru's terrible record for this type of assault with two words, *delincuencia* and *impunidad*.

I tried to organise replacement cards, but it proved so complicated that I decided to leave it until I returned to Sydney two months later, where I could make personal visits and local phone calls and claim the money stolen. No such guarantees existed for Antonio, who had to apply for a loan to cover the theft from his Peruvian debit card account, which he had one year to pay back, with interest.

'Do I run away, or stay and fight?'

I thought of our kidnappers and of the boys in Grade 6 at Colegio Elohim, some already as strong as men. Criminal gangs attracted such vulnerable youth as a substitute for the stable families they'd never had;

and I had been afforded a glimpse of what they may become if we couldn't provide them with another option through education. The decision took less than ten seconds. Of course I'd stay.

As an alternative to long-term rental, I began to think of purchasing a property, and when an apartment came up for sale right beside the Plaza Yanahuara, I bought it, for a tenth the price it would have fetched in Sydney. I imagined living in this expansive home with a foster family made up of the most neglected pupils of Colegio Elohim … a fantasy based firmly on ignorance of the reality of life in the slums. I failed to take into account that even the most neglected children already had parents, and no matter how much they suffered, they could only be removed from custody by judicial order.

Antonio enthused about my investment, its position, and its prospect to increase in value. I thought of his dingy little room, all the space I would have, and said to him suddenly, 'Why don't you move in too?'

'Soosanita, perhaps we should rent together first?'

'But I've already bought it.'

Of course he accepted, and with my relative first-world wealth, I forced a pivotal lifestyle decision with less deliberation than I'd give to choosing a new pair of running shoes.

I charged on, organising a new contract with the institute to begin work again in January of the following year. At the end of October, I headed off for eight weeks in Sydney to spend Christmas with my daughters. Meanwhile, Antonio would move himself and his few pieces of furniture into the apartment, so it would be ready when I returned to Arequipa to begin our live-in relationship.

I left to start my journey to Sydney in the middle of the day, when Antonio was teaching in classes, so I had no choice but to go alone to the airport by taxi. I rang and booked one, checked that the driver knew my name when he arrived, and sat in the front. Chatting to him from the outset, I hoped he wouldn't harm me if we'd shared a conversation, no matter how superficial, but this didn't prevent me from cringing, and clenching clammy palms when at one point we turned into a narrow street with high walls on either side. When we arrived safely at Departures, I climbed out with my bags and stood watching the small departing vehicle with a smile of relief. I'd made the ten-minute taxi ride without mishap; now I felt ready to breeze through the longest and most complicated international flight route.

Back in the Sydney December heat, I moved around the familiar kitchen, roasting turkeys stuffed with apricots and walnuts, to serve with salads, crusty bread, chilled champagne, and plum pudding with extra-strong brandy butter. We hosted two celebrations, one for my brother and his family, and one for my in-laws, serving it all out on long tables under umbrellas in the garden, where Katy had hung tinsel and colourful baubles over the grevilleas in the summer sunshine.

CHAPTER 15

Following that Christmas, which shone like a lighthouse beacon, an incoming tide of sadness and loss arrived within days. Katy's husband of three years had not been present at our celebrations, having stormed out of the house after an argument the day before. By the time I flew out of Sydney on December 30th, it had become clear that their marriage had hit serious problems; while Rachel, too, was miserable after a relationship break-up. I felt gutted, ripped in two, knowing my girls needed me, while Antonio waited impatiently in Arequipa.

The day dawned, and before leaving for the airport, I took Jack, the sweet-natured family dog, for a final walk through the bush by the harbour. I watched his white wagging tail as he skipped and sniffed, until tears smudged the eucalypt green all around me. At midday, Katy drove me to Mascot, where I resumed my sobbing and clung to her, trying to utter something helpful before, basically, leaving her to it. Still waving long after I lost sight of the car, I finally had to stop, turn around and push through the wide glass doors to begin my journey away from my daughter, when I wanted more than anything to stay by her side. Stumbling to the check-in, I handed over my passport and Peruvian residency card to the young lady, burst into tears again and blurted out to her, 'What are you supposed to do when you've got people you love on opposite sides of the globe? How do you reconcile two lives?' She could only smile sympathetically, hiding her thoughts, no doubt wondering if I was a security risk.

In transit at Auckland airport four hours later, my stomach churned with the acute awareness that I was still on the 'home' side of the Pacific. There was just time for an impulsive gesture, like Colin Firth's sudden-epiphany-Christmas-Eve-proposal dash from Gatwick to Marseille in *Love Actually* or Hugh Grant's last-minute-before-she-boards-to-leave-forever pursuit of Julia Roberts in *Notting Hill*. However I sat still, misery paralysing my urge to bolt to the ticket counter with my new credit card and leap onto the next plane back to Sydney. Finally came the call to board for the twelve-hour flight across a vast ocean. I picked up my hand luggage and joined the queue. Tanned olive faces, striking dark eyes, stylish scarves and ties, leather and gold accessories quickly surrounded me with the emphatic sounds and gestures of South American Portuguese and

Spanish, bearing me inexorably towards another continent, another life.

★

I flew east, so it was still the morning of New Year's Eve, local Arequipa time, when I made my way down the steps from the plane. I found Antonio waiting to escort me to our new home and kissed him wearily, murmuring about the tiring journey. We arrived at 301/808 Francisco Mostajo and he made me a cup of tea. Sitting in the sunny back room, we exchanged late Christmas presents, concentrating our conversation on their contents rather like polite strangers. He could not have been encouraged by my brittle smile and moist eyes as I tried to hold onto my tears, listening to news of his family, not trusting myself to speak about my own. I avoided his searching gaze as I stared out instead over the volcanoes, filling awkward silences with admiring exclamations at the view. Finally, he put his arms around me and kissed me; but as he led me to the bedroom, my mind and heart lurched to a pink house on the other side of the globe where two girls suffered, and their mother wasn't around.

I regained some self-control by the evening for our visit to his friends' place to see in the New Year. Coloured lights had been strung all over the dining and living room for Christmas, and European figures in a snow-covered nativity scene dominated a table of sparkling seasonal decorations. Pisco flowed freely from the outset, and at about 10 pm our host, who spent several months each year away from his family working in Switzerland as a chef, produced delicious paella and cake, which Antonio hardly touched. By midnight, we stood in the back garden and watched as all over Arequipa red, orange, silver and golden fireworks fizzed through the cold night sky. Drinking steadily throughout the night, Antonio became first merry, then irritable, and finally earnest, making proclamations of love to me which I suspected were the pisco talking. A lift at the end of the night meant we didn't have to face the taxi problem – just risk of death by road accident with a driver way, way over the limit, as indeed was Antonio. We finally made it home and went to bed, where he fell asleep at once. I knew I snored and that he ground his teeth, but I hadn't counted on him unconsciously kicking and chasing me all over the mattress. At dawn, not having slept a second, I wondered for the first time if perhaps this hadn't been a mistake … but for the moment, I put it down to jet lag and hoped things would improve.

Antonio eventually awoke on New Year's Day with no ill-effects from, or much recollection of, the night before. But the restlessness of sharing a bed continued and the following fortnight of sleep-deprivation had me sitting cross-legged every morning before sunrise on the cold tile floor of the maid's room at the back of the flat. Palms upward, I chanted softly, 'All hail the Jewel in the Lotus', trying to ease my way into some sort of tranquillity.

Within days I returned to my morning dance class where I wiggled and wobbled to the Latin beat, watched Emilio, and forgot everything for an hour. When not teaching I threw myself into, of all things, planting flowers – in the window box of my third-floor Arequipeñan flat. The friendly gardeners at the club, no doubt wondering about the mad gringa, helped me collect leaves and grass clippings into enormous plastic bags which I heaved up the hill and three flights of stairs to mulch the delicate seedlings. This horticultural creativity somehow brought me closer in my heart to my garden in Sydney, and to my girls whom I'd deserted, far away on the other side of the world. For a while I could forget the trap I had set for myself when I decided to live in Arequipa with my Peruvian lover.

★

'Do you meditate?' a female voice called out in Peruvian-American-English.

I glanced up from my Sunday reading by the outdoor pool at the club to see an arm waving above a bobbing bathing cap. An elderly lady in the water, holding on to the side, had spotted the catchy title of my book, *Buddhism for Busy People*. As I marvelled at her eyesight, she climbed out, pulled off her cap and shook a short mop of grey-white hair. Sitting down, she fixed me with bright blue eyes and said, 'My name is Patricia Roberts.'

I smiled at her. 'I'm Susi.'

'I come from an Arequipeñan Catholic heritage,' she continued, 'but I have studied Taoism and the dance of Tai Chi. I practise the integration of Western religion and Eastern mysticism. When can we talk more?'

Over coffee later that week, she briefly told me her life story. Born into a wealthy town family, with one grandfather English and the other German, she had married an American and emigrated to the US, where over three decades, she'd published poetry collections in Spanish and English, raised two children, completed university studies, and worked in Hispanic communities and international justice; before finally returning to Arequipa to pursue spiritual studies.

'I hold practice and discussion meetings twice a week. Would you care to join us?'

I almost squealed in delight. Missing my meditation

group in Sydney, I had stumbled, or rather splashed, into an opportunity to fill the gap.

★

With the beginning of the academic year in March, I went back to my weekly three mornings at Colegio Elohim. The trip from our apartment to the school involved two combis, connecting at the Feria Altiplano marketplace. Antonio took me on a trial run to show me where to change, but on my first morning I would have missed the stop without the enormous steel arches rising high up above the intersection to help me get my bearings. I called out to stop the combi as I spotted them looming. The conductor helped me down the metal steps and onto the street. 'Gracias,' I said, and with obvious surprise he replied that it was a pleasure, 'De nada, Señora.'

Not many passengers took the time to greet these individuals who worked twelve-hour shifts, heaving the heavy door, leaping on and off, calling out the litany of stops till they were hoarse, often forced to hang on outside the crowded vehicle as it hurtled through the traffic. Some too young, others too old, all too poor, they earned a pittance with no job security from one day to the next. Elohim's most neglected students would most likely end up in this work once they left the safety of the school.

I found my way to a brand new pedestrian crossing and waited until the luminous green man started walking. This one speeded up as the seconds counted down from twenty-five, until by 'two' and 'one' he sprinted at Olympic speed. Feeling an urge to pull at someone's sleeve and point to see if they shared the joke … I didn't, and hurried to the kerb.

The market bustled. On my left, brightly-coloured fruit and vegetables arranged on stands inside the building; to my right, those vendors who took their chances each day on the pavement. Paying no rent, they charged lower prices, everything they needed for the day's work fitting into roomy striped carry-alls: produce, display shelves, a wad of plastic bags, a hand-held balance for weighing, and a stool to sit on. Buyers clustered around a fruit stall of peaches, limes, mangoes, apples and bananas. Alongside, tomatoes, carrots, broccoli and dozens of different kinds of potatoes, abundant here in their country of origin; round yellow, tubular pinky-purple, oval dark brown, small grey and pitted black. Sellers kept watch, ready to pack up fast if the usually-relaxed police chose today to move them along.

Further on, a traditional mamacha from Puno in her hat, plaits and skirts, put the final touches to her stack of soft, round yellow cheeses. Wicker baskets, deep and wide as baths, groaned with triangular pan de trigo, or wheat bread, puffy, crunchy rolls which still smelt of the woodfire they'd been baked over. 'Un sol por favor,' I said, and the smiling young woman handed over six in a plastic bag; two for Rosa, two for any children who'd missed breakfast, and two for me. As I took them to move on I noticed that a large box on the pavement next to the bread seller was wobbling. I stepped over to it and opened its flap to peer inside, expecting to see fluffy yellow chickens or ducklings. Two dark eyes appeared in the gloom, and my own widened as I made out a small child beaming up at me. No wonder Rosa was so adamant that early stimulation for infants was as vital as any primary level. She'd told me of babies carried on their working mothers' backs, swaddled in blankets, in darkness and silence, whether asleep or awake; and of their noticeably impaired development when they started school at five or six. As I waved at the little boy in the cardboard carton, I understood the urgency to begin an early stimulation class at school for little ones such as him before it was too late.

Small glass cabinets on wheels displayed fresh avocado and tomato rolls, blended juices, and oranges peeled in artistic stripes. Shoppers took time over the newspaper headlines pegged up along the fence, scrutinising words or simply pictures if they couldn't read, while the elderly seller dozed on her collapsible stool under a shady hat. A youth trundled his cart of quails' eggs, layer upon layer, speckled brown and green, which he shelled and served in a napkin; while the hens' variety piled up in cardboard trays around a girl who could scarcely see over the top, though I supposed she would sell them all by the afternoon.

Rounding the corner, I found an old lady on her stool on the cement selling bags of onions, carrots and garlic, for one sol a kilo. I presumed she had no pension and would work there until she was too frail to haul her sack of vegetables on her back. Hopefully she had family members who would take her in, and not leave her on the street from dawn till dusk with a begging cup, like others I had seen. I greeted her, taking out a coin for a bag of carrots. Her face lit up as she said, 'Que Dios la bendiga, Señora!'

I smiled and accepted her blessing.

CHAPTER 16

Just a few weeks later, the cook's spouse smashed several windows of Colegio Elohim's kitchen with his fists while in a drunken fury. Carolina, a petite, attractive young indigenous woman, would always greet me cheerfully as she prepared lunch, tending enormous pots of steaming lentils and pans of meat with onions on the stove in the kitchen – a leaky room without benches, sink or running water. At twenty-eight, she had three children at the school – a daughter and two sons – and her earnings helped provide for them, or so I assumed. She minded a shack nearby, living there in one room with her family, and a swarm of puppies and kittens.

Her little boys struggled with learning difficulties and frequent punch-ups in the playground, and their older sister Helena still wet her bed at age ten, confiding to Rosa that her parents often fought violently. Carolina's shrill temper certainly didn't help, but she had reason for her outbursts – the father of her children rarely worked, and had seduced an eighteen-year-old girl, leaving her pregnant and destitute. On this particular afternoon, he arrived home staggering drunk to find the shack empty and his lunch nowhere in sight, Carolina having been delayed washing up at Colegio Elohim after the end of classes. In a slobbering rage, he stormed into the deserted school yard, shouting something equivalent to, 'Where's my fuckin' food, you bitch!' He lurched over to the cookhouse, yelling, 'C'mon … I know you're in there!' and lunged at a pane. It cracked and shattered, and inside, Carolina grabbed her children and dived for cover. He punched out the second window, which exploded in a rain of shards. His hands covered in blood, he smashed against the glass a third time while his daughter and sons clung to their mother and screamed.

At that point, Rosa and two male teachers arrived, having rushed from a staff meeting. 'Get off our property at once,' ordered one of the men, 'or we'll call the police!'

Glaring at them, the dishevelled young man slunk away, and shortly afterwards, Carolina and her children emerged unharmed from the kitchen. The next day, her lip split and angry bruises swelling bluish round her eyes and across her cheeks, she tearfully promised Rosa he would pay for the damage he had caused – but we never saw a centavo. I'd have gladly covered the cost, but Rosa warned me of the inevitable wildfire of gossip about the rich gringa making handouts to her favourites.

Some months afterwards, I heard that Carolina was saving to build her own shack, and assumed she planned to leave her brutal husband. Rosa helped me organise a discreet 'loan' to complete the basic outer walls of the hut and a door as a safe shelter for herself and her children before the rains. But Carolina gave the money straight to her husband, who put it down as a deposit on a loan to buy himself a car – supposedly to earn a living as a taxista. He smashed it beyond repair weeks later, driving blind drunk, without a licence.

Some sombre truths were beginning to sink in … about the realities of life in the slums, and my inability to do anything about them.

Meanwhile, another domestic drama, albeit much milder than Carolina's situation, was unfolding at 301/808 Francisco Mostajo. After a month of wakeful nights, I had summoned all the tact I could and moved myself and my things into the second bedroom to enjoy my first undisturbed sleep for ages, leaving Antonio alone in the double bed. He no longer had to put up with my snoring, while I no longer spent the nights wondering if his front teeth could indeed crack, and where the next kick would come from. We both slept better, but this move marked the beginning of a long and painful journey of personal and cultural clashes.

In fact, I thought the second bedroom was far preferable, because it had an enclosed balcony and a partial view northeast towards El Misti, whose volcanic temperament consistently captivated me with changing moods and colours. The vista from the master suite where Antonio now slept alone was over a sprawl of scaffolding, cement and iron tubing sticking up from unfinished buildings as far as the eye could see.

'But, Soosanita,' gasped Antonio when I ventured my opinion, 'this is the main room where the señor of the house resides with his wife, with a view over the portal, the street, and the rest of the apartment. This is how we design in Peru.'

The 'Peruvian design' of the apartment also meant that the stunning view out over all three volcanoes could only be had from the tiny, high toilet window, and the third bedroom. The latter, I had decided on my first inspection of the flat, would be used not for sleeping but as a living and eating area; even though it was not at all convenient to the dark kitchen … which faced the inside well of the building, next to the interior nook which should have housed the dining table. When I stood in the street outside and studied our building, I could pick out our back windows unencumbered by curtains and bathed in sunshine ... while those of all the other flats were firmly shut off from light and the magnificent volcanoes by blinds or heavy drapes at all hours of the day and night.

The interior nook and the vast parquet-floored viewless interior which should have been divided up into eating, television viewing and salon areas of the apartment, I decorated with traditional woven hangings and clay jugs and pots. We scoured the markets for dried beans and lentils to fill empty bottles with layers of black, chestnut, green, white, yellow and orange, and platters with dried corn cobs in similar colours, which we arranged upon tables and shelves of straw and raw wood. Antonio dubbed these displays our 'Peruvian corners', and visitors invariably exclaimed at the unusual spaciousness, uncluttered by heavy, oversized dark furniture; although whether their utterances were of enthusiasm or horror I was never altogether sure.

Antonio and I met at a food festival, at a time when Peruvian cuisine's international reputation was growing, with chefs such as Gaston Acurio and Humberto Sato leading the charge from Lima. The popular cooking show *Aventuras Culinarias* featured the laid-back Gastoncito and his friends preparing everything from ceviche, fish pieces marinated in lemon juice, through rocotto relleno, hot red pepper stuffed with savoury mince, to pastel de papa, potato bake with lashings of butter, and chicharrón de chancho, the fried pork dish I was contemplating when I first met Antonio. As part of a speaking exercise in one of my classes at the institute, the students had come up with the names of twenty-five culinary specialities local to the Arequipa region alone.

A whole separate television show was devoted to the creation of luscious tortas loaded with manja blanca, like a creamy caramel, and tres leches, various cakes made of 'three milks'. Just down the hill at the Plaza Yanahuara, tourists consumed bucket loads of queso helado, a thick cream churned over ice in a display of age-old tradition. The frozen block arrived each morning around 8 am in a little yellow taxi, together with the authentic wooden barrel, and a young woman in jeans who set everything up, then popped into a shop to change into her pretty frilled traditional blouse and skirt. In quiet moments when not besieged by holiday-makers wanting to buy ice cream and take her photo, she'd take out her mobile phone from her apron for a quick call.

Despite all this culinary promise, within days of Antonio and I setting up home together, eating habits and customs had emerged as a serious stumbling block to our relationship. Fusión cuisine and culture may have been taking off in Lima, but not so in our province, and certainly not in our apartment.

As I already knew, lunch in Arequipa is traditionally cooked over a long period and served up seasoned with potatoes and rice or pasta. Fresh, local vegetables are cheap and readily available and usually become soup, or a small cooked aside to the main dish. Salads pose a health risk given the contamination of the soil and water, the closest reliable substitute being soltero de queso, cooked broad beans with white cheese, peeled tomato and raw onion, or palta rellena, avocado stuffed with chicken, corn and lashings of mayonnaise. I love fresh greens and lightly-cooked carrots, broccoli, beans and the like, and had long ago realised how contrary Peruvian tastes and customs were to my own. What's more, I also understood Antonio's appetite difficulties, but shared his optimism that we'd be able to minimise the impacts for the sake of our life as a couple.

Just days after my arrival in Francisco Mostajo, I cooked a dinner of chicken and vegetables to be ready at 7.30 pm with candles and a bottle of wine, knowing Antonio finished classes at 7 pm, and assuming he would be eager to come straight home. Then I waited, until he finally showed up at 8.45, laden with supermarket bags and other bits and pieces which he'd bought after work.

'Been shopping? What a shame, your dinner's cold,' I said, smiling through clenched teeth, adding silently, 'and so is mine.' He told me he wasn't hungry anyway.

Supermarkets, shops and businesses in Arequipa stay open until late for customers like Antonio, who have eaten a substantial late lunch and, in many cases, had a siesta, then gone back to work, often until 7 or 8 at night. They don't tend to store and re-heat food, so they'll shop several times a week for fresh ingredients. Those with jobs will most likely do so in the evening, eventually coming home to eat a snack in front of the television, the best programs beginning at 9.30 or 10 pm.

In contrast, over the twenty-odd years I had spent feeding four children and a husband three times a day in Australia, I'd shopped fortnightly, filling two trolleys in the supermarket, bringing it all home to store in the fridge, freezer and pantry. We ate a light breakfast, sandwiches or salad for lunch at work, and I used to unwind after a long day as I prepared a simple dinner of meat or fish, vegetables, and one carbohydrate to be eaten with the family around 7 pm.

After my first disastrous effort, I no longer even attempted to put together an evening meal to eat with Antonio. One night, he found me rummaging around in the fridge to see what I could prepare for myself. 'Soosan! Is this how you fed your children, with whatever you could find? Aye, Dios mío! Didn't you plan your meals? I used to work out the week's menu, go to the market, and buy the ingredients so the maid would know what to cook each day. Your family must have hated your cooking.' I stood stunned. I'd never faced such a tirade from him before, and wondered what could have triggered it. Did my past culinary skills, or lack thereof, matter so much?

Following the Peruvian middle-class custom, when first married, Antonio and his wife, both working full-time, put a sign in the window of their rented flat. They sought a live-in maid for domestic duties in return for food, board and a small salary. A young girl knocked on the door. She'd saved all she had to buy a one-way bus ticket to Arequipa from her village in the mountains outside Cusco ... and so they hired Florentina, who stayed in her own room in the house, cooked and cleaned, and minded children, for years. She eventually left to marry and set up a small restaurant using the savings and skills she had acquired during her time with them, but she still remained close to the family; indeed, as godfather to her children, Antonio helped put them through school and tertiary education – as did many folk for the families of their long-term resident employees.

Understanding and respecting this reality, all the same I caught myself muttering peevishly under my breath, 'What fun you must have had planning meals for Florentina to prepare when she wasn't washing your shirts, cleaning your house and minding your children.' The cavernous cultural gap loomed as I realised I could never answer his question and explain, let alone in castellano, that in Sydney one did not employ an indigenous live-in maid. So yes, each day I did open the fridge and pull out something suitable to cook the family for dinner (not lunch), and modern appliances – washing machine, microwave, freezer, dryer – plus hard-to-find babysitters, helped me perform the same duties as his home help.

Even when he'd lived alone after his divorce, Antonio had still bundled up his dirty clothes, underwear and socks and sent them off every week to Florentina, by then in her fifties and running her restaurant, to wash by hand, dry, iron where necessary and return. Things changed dramatically when I bought a little washing machine shortly after we moved in to Francisco Mostajo. We christened her Esmerelda and it was love at first sight as he watched her agitate, rinse and spin garments, towels and sheets to be hung out to dry on the airy balcony. Doing the laundry became his favourite pastime … and he told me Florentina was deeply offended when Esmerelda supplanted her.

CHAPTER 17

I forgot all our difficulties when Antonio's little child took over, shining out of his brown eyes as various expressions chased each other across his face. He'd wave his arms and prance around as he described the books he read voraciously as a youngster – classics in translation, *Isla del Tesoro*, *Ivanhoe*, *Tarzan* – and re-enacted for me the flights of fancy which transported him and his siblings to the worlds he created from their pages.

On one occasion, in the middle of a conversation about current affairs, he jumped up and single-handedly performed a scene from the day's national news which he followed avidly; an interview between reporters with microphones and a disgraced former Peruvian president found to own several mansions worth millions. 'Señor,' he began, 'can you confirm or deny for us the rumour that you purchased … ?' I giggled as he leapt sideways and took on the defiant expressions and defensive bumbling of the hapless ex-politician, 'My mother-in-law bought them!' – trying to talk his way out of the insinuations by the polite, eloquent and persistent interviewers (back on their side) firing questions into his face. 'But Señor, doesn't she live on an old age pension in Israel?'

True to his proud roquero identity, Antonio would belt out rock 'n roll with almost all the words right, thanks to his time in the US on an American Field Scholarship in 1968; after which he'd embraced hippy-ism, grown a Bob Marley halo and got into the bohemian scene Arequipa-style. When a favourite romantic ballad came on to the radio, he'd pull me up to swirl joyfully around the kitchen, and I'd move effortlessly with him as if it were the most natural thing in the world.

But after that first outburst about my cooking, I began to notice how often his sunny mood could change to aggression and hostility, particularly later in the evenings. Remembering my volatile temper and track record, I'd wonder guiltily what I'd said.

'Aye, Soosan, why do you turn on the thermostat in the evenings?' Antonio demanded.

I used it in the kitchen at Francisco Mostajo, con-trary to the Peruvian custom, which is to make do with cold water, meaning that many houses don't have a hot tap over the sink.

'To wash the dishes properly,' I said.

'Oh, so you gringos don't think we're clean enough?'

Next came the power bill. My four children would attest to my obsession about teaching them to save electricity while they were growing up, nagging them to turn lights off every time they left their rooms. I'd run around the house muttering and flicking switches, blowing a fit one day when Lisa, in a panic because she'd run out of knickers, had put one pair all alone in the dryer. One Arequipeñan evening, Antonio lectured me about the extravagance of gringos, and he should know because of 'mi prima, my cousin who lives in London and came to stay at our house once, and every night she left it lit up like a birthday cake, lights on in every room. We Peruvians are not so wasteful as you, we can't afford to be, of course; we're used to going without.' The rise in the bill which had prompted this extraordinary speech had in fact had been due to my re-adjusting the timer so he could have a hot shower after his run on his new timetable. I did not react, but went into his room, and found the computer, CD player, and three separate lights all on … and nobody home.

Of course we couldn't agree on TV programs, which meant that I would often go to bed at 9 pm to escape some violent blood-spattering Argentinean crime series; or he would come home to find me engrossed in *Lord of the Rings* for the fiftieth time on the DVD and retreat to his lair, feeling the same way about my choice as I did about his. In the end he bought me another TV as a Mother's Day gift.

We also battled over his rainbow-striped folding easy chair. He would put it out in the middle of the back room we had adopted as our dining-living room to watch TV, and I would find it there the next morning cluttering up the breakfast space. No matter how hard I tried to ask him politely to put it away, my bristling fury and desire to hurl it out of the window would sound through my words, and he would respond in kind.

I began to wonder if perhaps we had both been independent, and stubbornly so, for far too long.

'Feel the spark of energy from the universe.'

Patricia stood in her garden, arms raised, El Misti behind her above cultivated terraces. As on every Tuesday and Thursday morning, I'd caught the combi to her house to join her with a group of five other women, watching and imitating, as she performed several rituals of Tai Chi. She continued her commentary with the movements.

'While you feel the power from above, know also that you are firmly rooted in the earth. Heaven-Earth. Wheel vertically and connect the polarities.'

My body stretched and I rotated my arms, up to the heights, down to the depths, thinking of my past life, four busy children, husband, and stressful careers.

'Action–Non Action, Yang–Yin.'

Speak, or stay silent; interfere, or do nothing; punish, or turn a blind eye; argue the point, or let it go. If only I'd done things differently. Taken more time to listen and reflect.

'Bring it all into your centre, open the furnace and release it as fire to the mountains, the Apus gods. Offer your life with all its imperfections.'

Flames raced from my outstretched arms towards the mighty volcano.

'Immediately feel the rain coming down. Receive it, let it soak you to your roots, and become your energy.'

A comforting image, the water of absolution … pardoning myself.

'Grow branches like a tree, turn and feel the breeze. Observe everything, do not shy away from pain.'

Memories circling, set off by the movement, and by Patricia's voice.

'Face the front again. With a sweep of your arm, collect from right and left your treasures. Hold them.'

In my hands, goals, attitudes, achievements and opinions …

'Feel their weight, pulling you down, making you heavy, not free.'

I had always thought they moved me on in life, but

now I realised how much they restricted my freedom to choose.

'Let them go into the earth.'

'Twa!' I breathed out, opening my hands as if dropping an immense weight.

'Trust that at the right moment they'll return.'

One day, as we reached this point, a hummingbird flitted into the tree before me; scarcely larger than a grasshopper, with a long feather tail swishing from side to side, balancing it vertically as it plunged its long beak into a blossom, before darting to the next. The distinctive 'ts, ts,' call came as a second tiny creature hovered outside the foliage; then the two of them danced off together in the morning light.

Nature had offered her message – our needs will be met at the appropriate time, though not always as expected. The birds knew this, but, as a human, I struggled to envisage the resolution of the difficulties of 301/808 Francisco Mostajo. Would I eventually escape? And, to use an appropriately local metaphor, how much water would have to flow down the Rio Chili and under the Puente Grau bridge before I did?

'No hay profesores!' Rosa moaned at Colegio Elohim, where by mid-March, she still hadn't filled all staff positions although the school term was already underway. The issue would arise every year as teachers waited for better offers before finally committing. Often not until several weeks after the pupils had returned would Rosa manage to fill all academic positions with professionals prepared to support not only the children, but also many of the parents as they battled against high odds.

One of these, Alicia, young mother of a Grade 4 boy and a toddler, worked in the kitchen alongside Carolina, chopping onions and potatoes. She earned enough to gradually and single-handedly construct a hut while her abusive husband languished in jail for robbery with assault. Around them bustled Señora Maria, one of our true success stories, labouring over stews and rice, always efficient and dependable. Her two young sons attended Elohim, while her daughter, having already graduated from primary at the school, had started secondary college in an outer suburb down the hill. She planned to go on to university, all supported by Señora Maria in the kitchen, and her husband, labouring equally hard on building sites.

One morning after class I spoke to Isabella, the Grade 2 Teacher, one of a handful who had stayed beyond twelve months to continue working at Colegio Elohim steadfastly over many years. I asked her what inspired her.

'I am called as a teacher, and I try to give my pupils some relief from the reality I know they are living

…' her voice caught, '… the childhood I survived.' Fighting tears, she forged on, her eyes seeking mine in a plea for understanding. 'I went to the local public school where the teachers told me I had a choice, the right road or the wrong road, and I didn't have to turn into my parents. This is the message I try to give to my own classes … don't turn into your parents.'

I waited for several seconds, before asking softly, 'Did any person in your family support you?'

'No-one, but I used to escape onto the roof of our shack and stare up at the night sky, at the stars.'

One day, an email arrived from Richard with news of his engagement. A vivid image popped into my head. A Susi-faced mechanical Luna Park clown, mouth open wide for the public to shoot pellets at, slowly turning away, and then, driven relentlessly by its motor, back again, still grinning, for the next assault.

It evaporated when I remembered his partner's treatment for breast cancer two years previously.

Just days later, Katy told me over the phone of her husband's acrimonious departure after she had finally told him to leave. 'I feel so much better, Mum, as if a bag of concrete has been lifted off my back.'

I heard the relief in her voice, and let go of a small part of my own guilt, at least for the moment.

★

Over Easter, Antonio and I put on a united front for Peter's arrival from London with his girlfriend for a two-week visit. I waved on the airport observation deck as I spotted my son's tall, familiar form striding across the tarmac, his face turned up and breaking into a grin when he saw me for the first time in a year. Antonio had moved into the maid's quarters to welcome the young couple into the comfort of the main suite, and they responded readily to his charm. Peter and I caught up on family news, and he travelled out with me to Colegio Elohim. I translated as he chatted to Rosa, and on his visits to the classes, he patiently allowed little people to climb all over him, fascinated by his height, his blue eyes and his closely shaved fair hair.

'There's poverty and despair in the slums of London, too,' he said on the way home. 'It's just in a different form.'

'You don't have to travel far to find suffering,' I murmured.

I took the young couple to Cusco and across the Bolivian border to Copacabana on the shores of Lake Titicaca. Catching the boat to the Isla del Sol, we walked its length in sunshine, stopping for a picnic overlooking eucalypts and turquoise waters, finally checking into a charming little local hotel near the wharf. That evening, at sunset, against a background of mountains across the silver water, Peter walked with his beloved to the top of a hill and asked her to marry him.

We returned to Arequipa and travelled to Colca Canyon. In those last few days of their visit, watching them together, the unease which had niggled me ever since they'd arrived finally snowballed into real concern about their compatibility. Antonio felt the same way. Just two months before, Katy had ended her marriage. As Peter and his new fiancée boarded the plane back to London, I farewelled them with a sinking feeling, wishing I could somehow shield my son from the pain I sensed was heading his way.

CHAPTER 18

Months passed, and the three mornings at Colegio Elohim, two with Patricia, and the usual sessions at the institute, kept me busy and minimised the time spent at home. By the middle of the year, Antonio and I had ended up leading separate lives. We'd get up at different times, spend the day apart, prepare and eat our own meals, and at day's end go to our individual rooms. I had no idea what he might have been doing every evening behind his closed door as, with nothing else to do, I read in bed and went to sleep. If I woke later, though, I always noticed that his light remained on into the early hours of the morning. When I asked him, he told me he was reading, but on one or two occasions I peeped in and found him fast asleep, so flicked the switch.

'I backed up everything on an external hard drive, but then I couldn't think where to hide it, so it's under the bed.' Peter grinned sheepishly at me over Skype from London. He'd been telling me about a robbery across the road from his house and his attempts to safeguard his own data just in case. Although I regularly backed up my files, the conversation got me thinking again about my passport and credit cards. Since the kidnap, I always left them at home, but perhaps I needed to conceal them. Over the following days I scoured the apartment for a foolproof spot, and when I found it, duly secreted away my money belt and its contents.

Not two weeks later, I arrived home just after dark to find Antonio crouched in a chair, leaping up when he saw me, mumbling and trying to prevent me from going any further into the flat.

'What? What's happened?' I glanced back at the front door, only then taking in the broken lock and splinters of timber, and pushed past him to my bedroom. I turned on the light and my eyes flew over a scene of rampage. The mattress upended, bedding sent flying, pillows removed from cases and flung away, every drawer wrenched open and contents scattered all over the place. I scanned the empty desk, my stomach sinking as I frantically searched my memory in the hope that I'd left my laptop somewhere else that morning. But it was gone, together with all my sentimental dress jewellery from Nepal which I had kept in a shelf in the closet. I ran to my hiding place. The money wallet was still there, undiscovered.

Arriving home after work, Antonio had heard a noise as he reached our landing, but before he'd had time to react, three figures had charged past him down the stairs. He'd rushed after them, but fortunately for him, had not caught them. They had easily broken our apartment's lock and entered, but as we surveyed the damage it became clear they had gone straight to my room, not even entering his, or the living areas. How had they got into the building? Had they come directly up to the third floor to our flat, or had they tried other doors? None bore any marks; they all had elaborate bars and barriers, but these were not visible from the outside so how did the intruders know our lock was the only inadequate one in the building? And the question which hovered unspoken; did they know that a gringa lived in apartment 301? Perhaps our elderly neighbour had accidentally left the catch of the main security door unlatched; it had happened before. Or perhaps someone had let them in. Our concierge was a young man who spoke little and moved quietly. Or did he watch, and move stealthily? The telephone company had come to repair the line the previous day; the two technicians had spent an hour in my room ...

Once again, I remembered Antonio's words after my street attack. 'Someone will always be watching you.' I began to glance twice at anyone near our apartment block talking on a mobile phone, to harbour doubts about the caretaker, to wonder about the repairmen. I upbraided myself for being paranoid, but it seemed that nowhere was safe. In the street, in a taxi, in the combi where I had been pickpocketed more than once, and now, even in my own home.

One last fond ritual which remained for Antonio and me was *adobo*, an Arequipeñan tradition which begins every Sunday around 5 am. Small restaurants and many private homes put out an earthenware pot of pork stewed in corn beer over coals on the pavement, filled to the brim and bubbling enticingly. We still occasionally strolled mid-morning to a local rustic picantería restaurant, to spend a precious hour sitting on a wooden bench under a whitewashed stone arch ceiling, chatting comfortably, his arm around my waist, his eyes laughing into mine. We'd watch the boisterous family groups around us, parents talking volubly, children slurping up every last drop soaked into crisp white bread wiped around the porcelain bowl. After the traditional shot of anis liqueur to 'kill the pig', we'd walk home again, and there our companionable interlude ended, as Antonio retired to his room for his midday siesta, a concept completely alien to me. I'd wander around the flat at a loss, eventually resorting to re-varnishing furniture. I couldn't face the idea of painting walls or making much-needed improvements to the place. Somehow I knew, or perhaps just wished, that I wouldn't be there for much longer. At times I'd yearn to reach out and touch Antonio's face … but the few special moments we could still share, stood out against the backdrop of our long, lonely weeks in an emotional desert as barren as the hills around Arequipa.

In September, clicking on a friend's Facebook notification, I saw dozens of snaps of Richard's wedding. I sat numb, wondering what else this year could deliver.

CHAPTER 19

My jaw dropped. 'How old did you say he was, Rosita?'

Sunlight poured through the open door into the hot, windowless cubicle Rosa used as an office. We were going over more of the early history of the school under the control of the elderly gringo and his mission. Four teachers had been hired, but over time their salaries had begun to dwindle until the gringo had finally announced that the funds had dried up. Rosa had just told me that she'd wondered at the time about his young Peruvian secretary, who was also his lover, who controlled the finances and was jealous because he was interested in someone else.

She paused to answer my question. 'At that point, he'd have been over eighty.'

My mouth stayed open in a fish gape as her tale unfolded like a Mexican telenovela. A lawyer was called in and discovered the college had been registered in the name of the charity the elderly gringo supposedly represented. The lawyer instructed that Colegio Elohim be handed over to Rosa, so she could sell it to recover the wages owed to her and the teachers. As I squinted out of the gloom up at the buzzing flies and dust particles swirling in the sunlit doorway, I wondered who, exactly, he thought would buy it.

Meanwhile, the elderly gringo ditched the secretary to marry his Peruvian Spanish teacher, sixty years his junior, and they vanished with all the money siphoned off donations meant for Colegio Elohim. I imagined tabloid headlines if they ever got hold of the story, 'No fool like an old fool … octogenarian missionary flees with the floozy and the funds.' Undaunted, Rosa, Sylvia and Yulissa decided to battle on, and form the Asociación Vida y Esperanza, a not-for-profit named for 'Life and Hope', to run the school as a charity. They contracted another Arequipeñan lawyer, member of a local Christian church who had worked with foreign missionaries, to set it up ethically.

But the havoc wreaked by the elderly gringo did not end there. In his haste to be gone, he failed to pay an outstanding bill to his actuary. When Rosa went to the public land registry to list her organisation as owner of the school, she discovered that the accountant had placed an embargo on exactly half of the college's property as revenge for his unpaid fees. This action meant that nothing could be done to the land, nor its four cheap, flimsy classrooms, until the ban could be lifted when the elderly gringo paid his dues.

Rosa told me of the groups of genuine people she'd come in contact with over the years who'd done everything they could to help keep the school afloat, of the international Christian charity which had assumed responsibility for the cost of the daily lunches, and continued its support despite global financial chaos. And of Jimmy, who had channelled contributions to the salaries through his dental clinic until finally announcing that there was no more money.

She turned to me and smiled. 'And then you came from far away, supported by your friends with their warm hearts.'

'And we have a second-storey roof ... on the block we do, indisputably, own,' I said brightly, fully aware that in shifting focus away from my private life, the children and teachers of Colegio Elohim had given me far more than I could ever give them.

In October, a generous donation arrived from an Australian benefactor. I deposited it into the account of the Asociación Vida y Esperanza and the following week construction of a new wing began. An army of strong, stocky builders descended on the makeshift kitchen and Rosa's tiny office, belting at them with mattocks until they collapsed in a cloud of furious insects. A massive earthmover began pounding at the rock to prepare the foundations. I watched the flimsy brick building right on our border shuddering and shaking, imagining the glee with which the neighbours would sue for damages when it fell down. However, it stood firm, and the construction continued in a whirl. Thin wooden saplings went up as scaffolding; several small concrete mixers appeared, together with women to pour in cement, sand, gravel and water. As usual they brought their toddlers, who splashed around in the mud while their mothers heaved to attach long hoses to the communal tap. Dilapidated trucks arrived, laden with locally-made red bricks and metres and metres of steel rods to reinforce the thick slab roofing essential for this seismic region so close to the volcano.

In town, such activity would have rendered the area off-limits to the public, but up in the hills of Cenepa, doubled-up grades crowded into the remaining class-rooms to continue the last months of the school year alongside the dust, the whacking of the digger, and the grinding of the cement mixers. Adding to the din, the builders hammered and sawed, shouting to each other over the reggaetón belting out of their radios. Through it all, children and teachers alike watched, boggle-eyed, as their new school took shape.

Buoyed by the progress of the building, I allowed myself to hope that no more nasty surprises lay in store and the following year would lead my life to a better place. 'Not so fast,' a little voice warned.

Sure enough, over two days in early November, I received four emails from my Sydney neighbours, full of understanding for the difficult situation and not wanting to worry me, but, honestly, the level of raucous partying next door had gone beyond reasonable limits. I rang and spoke to Lisa, suggesting that maybe I should pay a visit.

'No, Mum,' she said, 'if you come and try to lay down the law, it'll make everything a hundred times worse. Leave it with me; I'll soon have it under control.'

'Okay, darling, but let me know if you need me and I'll be there in a flash,' I said, sensing that I wasn't going to get any more information. After that, the neighbourhood cyberspace airways went quiet, offering me little idea what might have been going on.

'Susita,' began my Danish friend Anja the social worker some weeks later over morning tea in the back room of Francisco Mostajo. Her face creased in concern. 'I have known Antonio for some time and of course I care for you deeply as my friend,' she began in English. Despite her ruse to improve our castellano when we'd first met in the hostel, she had long ago revealed her perfect mastery of my mother tongue, but only used it when she wanted to be absolutely sure I understood. I sensed something serious was coming. 'I think he has a problem.' She hesitated, choosing her words, '… of alcohol addiction. I've worked with many such cases, and the signs are unmistakable.'

I stared at her, trembling from the depth of my stomach. Of course he drank far too much on far too many occasions – which I knew and hated – but what was she saying? That he was drinking behind my back at home? Through my mind flashed his mercurial changes of temper, his outbursts, his frequent visits to the bathroom, his closed door with the light on late at night. Anja had first commented months before that I was losing weight, and I'd taken her into my confidence, sharing with her Antonio's moods, my reactions, and our escalating arguments, always blaming myself and my temper. I had never before knowingly encountered alcoholism; my naïveté was absolute.

As I thought more and more about it over the following weeks, I said nothing to Antonio. To my own horror, I started rifling through clothes in closets and drawers, searching for hidden bottles; but I never found them. Racked with doubt, I revisited our 'cultural differences', and the clashes they seemed to cause. But without concrete proof, I couldn't be absolutely sure … perhaps I was imagining it all and doing him a terrible injustice.

Finally, after yet another heated argument, he

stormed out of Francisco Mostajo with a backpack. My heart sank – but within hours, relief was flooding through me. Alone at last, as usual I prepared to run, seeing a way out and away from this situation. As soon as possible, I'd sell the flat and everything in it once he removed his things, finally salvaging my freedom to choose … and never, ever would I give it up again. That same night, I wrote him a letter, thanking him for the times we'd had, adding that I hoped we could still be friends and meet occasionally, intending to deliver it to his locker at the institute the following week.

Twenty-four hours later, he appeared at the flat, ready to return and pretend nothing had happened. Amazed, I refused. 'But it was just a moment,' he said, in his adorable Peruvian-lilting voice. 'It's all forgotten.'

'Until the next time.' I realised I had murmured the same response Richard had repeated over the years of our marriage.

I asked Antonio to leave, only weeping once the door had closed behind him.

A week passed and I invited him back to talk things over. 'I know I have caused you much pain, mi Soosanita. I will do everything I can to change,' he said, sitting beside me on the sofa, head bowed. No longer confronted with the nightly transformation of his personality when we lived under the same roof, I saw before me the dear man I loved, inhaled his minty smell, and felt his warmth. 'You're still my girl,' he said softly, and I began to cry, hugged him, and sank into his arms, surrendering with relief to the soothing idea that things would be different.

He rented a room a few blocks away. We went out to lunch every weekend, often returning to the flat for a romantic interlude before he went home. Save the odd phone call, we lived our own lives in between. I didn't ask to share his secrets, nor he mine. For the moment, it seemed to work.

In December I left the institute, never to return. I had lasted exactly twenty-four months, double my original contract, but despite the polite charm of the young adults, keen intelligence of the children, and my own adequate performance – I'd loathed the work. All the same, I had made many lasting friendships and, of course, found love. Without the employment contract I had been offered there, I would never have given up my career in Australia to travel to Arequipa, leaving my life so much the poorer.

No longer with a paying job in Peru, I had to give up my Carné Extranjería, the residency card I had struggled so hard to obtain, meaning my visits from then on would be as a tourist and restricted to six months.

CHAPTER 20

Ten days into the New Year, still underweight and stressed after the events of the previous twelve months, I fainted one morning outside my apartment in Francisco Mostajo and fell hard onto concrete. I awoke surrounded by concerned neighbours and tried to tell them I was all right ... until I felt sticky blood at the back of my head. They called the local community ambulance which took me to the clinic where I had six stitches. Four days later the wound seemed dry and almost healed, and I couldn't wait to return to dance with Emilio.

That night, I woke up at 3 am in a dark, spinning vortex which got worse with every movement of my head. I levered myself into sitting position and stared at a street lamp until eventually the room stilled. There I remained, terrified, wondering whom I could contact. At dawn, I reached for my mobile phone and rang Antonio.

He came straight over and took care of me all day, organising a mountain of pillows at bedtime to keep me upright – and spending the night in his old room, to be close when I woke up nauseated. He ended up staying a week – then two – finally moving back into the flat, shepherding me to doctors' appointments as I struggled to overcome the initial dizziness and reach a level of manageable daily activity. I'd ease myself carefully into bed at night and lie rigid, afraid to move my head to the left or the right, let alone turn over, or relax into sleep; swimming became a challenge rather than the pleasure it had always been, mat stretch exercises impossible, and dance a sorry, stiff state of affairs. Not to mention the dentist's drill, as I endured twenty fillings, root canal therapy and three gold crowns over the following twelve months.

Although the vertigo gradually abated, over time several relapses, in Arequipa and elsewhere, threw me back into a cold sweat, forcing me to start all over again. I learned that microscopic particles in my ear canal had been dislodged, and I mastered exercises to 'tip' and reposition them when the dizziness recurred. The condition and my dread of it remained with me for four years until the physical symptoms finally disappeared and the fear left me in peace. I knew I had recovered when an earthquake in Chile caused the strongest tremor of my experience in Arequipa, the walls shuddering at midnight until I leapt out of bed, grabbed my passport and raced outside. Surfing on the ground as it shifted beneath my feet, I felt a surge of guilty relief that it was the earth moving and not a relapse of the vertigo.

In mid-March, two months after the accident, the grand opening of Colegio Elohim's new wing took place. With a crowd of excited children in tow, Rosa and I moved up and down staircases through an entire new wing of freshly-painted classrooms with tiled floors, a spacious administration area, and toilet blocks; cutting ribbons as students crowded to get into photo after photo snapped by the teachers. Construction had continued during the holidays in January and February, thanks to a mild rainy season with no more than a few showers, and Rosa and her husband Juan had stretched the budget to include inside finishes and floors – all for the cost of a bathroom renovation in a Sydney home. The euphoria of that day returns whenever I walk up the dusty road to Colegio Elohim and see girls and boys on the upper verandahs waving and calling out to me over the desert hills.

Despite the vertigo, I had to travel that year, to Sydney for Rachel's 21st birthday party and then to Greece for Peter's wedding. Antonio remained in the flat to guard against burglary, as properties left unattended for long periods invariably ended up ransacked.

The arrangement suited us both, as I had neither the time nor emotional energy to organise selling or letting it out commercially, and he was delighted to return to his comfortable room for another year; especially, I suspected, without me there for most of it. So practical convenience stalled the status of our relationship, and its problems remained on hold.

At the end of April, I arrived back in Sydney. Katy, now free and single, had become the wild teenager she'd never allowed herself to be when growing up as the responsible older sister, and she threw parties to match. Lisa, who'd been the rebellious adolescent, had taken on the role of mother, trying to keep things under control. Meanwhile, Rachel, attempting to study full-time at university and hold down a bar job, suffered in silence. No wonder nobody wanted to tell me anything, or less, invite me to return.

In the garden under a marquee, Rachel's 21st featured the usual finger food, alcohol, music and fun … until about one in the morning, when the invited parents went home and left me to it, with seventy or so inebriated young adults. At 4.30 am I stood in the still-floodlit, finally deserted garden, ankle-deep in cold, sodden grass which stank of alcohol, my thongs squelching, my hands in rubber gloves. As I fished out broken glass to throw into recycling bins, the odd drunken shout pierced the silence from a leftover group in the street outside waiting for a taxi. I paused to look up at the modern two-storey back façade of the house which had been our family home since Richard and I had bought it nearly thirty years before.

The inside lights were on, illuminating the spacious eating-living area, but I gazed beyond it, back in time, to the gloom of the original kitchen. I watched myself, four weeks pregnant with Katy, opening the enamel door of the antique oven, struggling not to throw up as a stench of gas billowed out and swamped the aroma of the quiche. In the musty old dining room of our renovator's dream, our parents sat on camp chairs at a folding table, awaiting their first lunch. My mum sat the head, facing the wooden seat of the toilet opposite, as I'd forgotten to shut the door to the bathroom where the cracked bath tub sat beneath the light-it-and-duck gas water heater over the single tap.

Images flew past of Richard and me, ripping linoleum off the floor of the timber addition at the back, discovering newspapers laid beneath it, featuring images tracking the final stages of construction of the arches of the Harbour Bridge. The two sides inched towards each other in every successive edition over eight months, but never met, as the flimsy extension was completed shortly before the final joining on 19 August 1930. I remembered feeling Katy kicking as I watched the plumber connect mains hot water to our new kitchen and washing machine, just days before her arrival. Then two years further on, the jungle cleared out of the back garden where I now stood, we brought baby boy Peter home, bellowing his appreciation for the bunches of flowers arranged all over the house.

I stared up from the garden to the dining room window and recalled Lisa as a curly blonde toddler, standing on 'her' chair, watching the mini-caterpillar digging the foundations for the second renovation, while her tiny sister Rachel slept in a crib in the middle of a construction site. Once again I heard the builder answering the phone, 'Sorry love, she can't talk now – she's breastfeeding the baby.'

As the kids had grown into partying, this house had hosted its fair share of riotous events, particularly on New Year's Eve, given the view of the Sydney fireworks from the harbour peninsula just down the road. Traditionally, on that night anyone, in any state, knew they were welcome to sleep over rather than try to make their way home. One year a young man arrived at the door clearly tired and emotional at 4.30 am, when the house was already full of bodies strewn all over the sofas and floors in every room. The only bedding left was a bath mat which I handed over and settled him into the last corner where he curled up and passed out with a beatific smile upon his face.

I sighed, shifting my feet submerged in the beer-drenched grass. Without parents around, everything had changed. This party was over and thankfully the police hadn't been called, no serious accidents had occurred, nothing had burned down or blown up ... but I couldn't risk a repeat performance, especially in my absence. Not only for the safety of the guests and welfare of the neighbourhood, but also because the house was my part of the divorce settlement; I depended on it for my future. The time had come ... the only sensible course was to sell.

That same afternoon – once everyone had finally woken up and extraneous non-family members had wandered off – I broke the news to the girls. They agreed it was time they all moved out ... but I feared that the deep-down effects of the wrench away from their home, the last remnant of the nuclear family they'd once belonged to, would drive deep and last long. As would my guilt.

I returned to Arequipa for just six busy weeks, then set off again in early July to meet my daughters in London. From there we flew out to attend Peter's wedding on Kefalonia Island, a pretty paradise of whitewashed villages draped with crimson and yellow bougainvillea set in the tranquil waters of the Ionian. Packed with tattooed, lobster-red tourists, it offered tavernas, Zorba-dancing waiters, white sandy bays, translucent waters, bus tours, cruises and all-night discos.

Richard came alone, and we shared family moments

together without awkwardness. Peter married his sweetheart on a sheltered beach in evening sunshine, with his sisters, his parents, and her mother present, all of us barefoot in the warm sand. We celebrated afterwards on a restaurant balcony with a view over the water, beneath green foliage and purple grapes, toasting the couple from carafes of fruity red wine served with vine rolls, tender lamb and fresh fish. I relaxed into thinking that perhaps my fears about their future together had been misplaced ...

September found me once again bound for Sydney, with one object in mind – to prepare the family home for sale. Katy having already left, I moved back into the main bedroom, then spent a month cleaning and airing to get ready for the open inspections. When I'd finished, everything was arranged as it had been during the first year after Richard's departure, a fitting way to farewell the home which had sheltered me through the initial trauma. I left it spotless for each viewing, walking to the local café with Jack the dog to sip and relax while he sat patiently under the table. The date for the auction arrived, the house sold, just, and then came time to empty it.

Every item of furniture the girls didn't want I advertised on the internet, and watched with satisfaction as my possessions left to begin life all over again in new hands. Couples with babies took the pieces I had restored for my own children years before. Mum's sewing machine went to a father for his daughter, her dinner set to a husband for his wife's thirtieth, the sitting-room armchairs to a smart professional couple. My English oak desk, which had once been a table in Dad's naval cabin, was assigned to an antique dealer. A keen hobby carpenter bought the tool bench, while a young family claimed the garden umbrella and furniture for their brand new home. The broken iron-lace table was snapped up by an elderly handyman to restore for his granddaughter, the clay pots by an avid gardener who drove over one hundred kilometres to pick them up. The dressing table became the property of a new mother, and I donated the bulky dining-room chairs to my meditation group. I felt liberated, a comfortable fit with my growing sense of detachment from material clutter. Things I couldn't sell, I left out on the verge in the age-old Australian tradition, and they all disappeared overnight. It soothed me to see a cycle beginning all over again.

Lisa left first. I stood alone in the street long after the line of vehicles had disappeared, her friends providing transport to a share-house. In the middle of a storm on the afternoon before Rachel's departure, I heard a scream from her bedroom and arrived to find her staring at the paving outside where a currawong had pounced on a dove and was ripping the gentle bird's throat out with its cruel beak. Within moments the rain had washed away the blood, tiny brittle bones and feathers, leaving no trace of the slaughter except the tears on our cheeks. The following grey, drizzly day I waved my youngest daughter off with her own convoy of four-wheel drives, borrowed by loyal companions from their parents. As Rachel left the home she'd lived in all her life, I felt my heart filling with concrete.

The evening before the hand-over of the house, I invited Richard for a final drink. As we sat on the two remaining plastic chairs in the bare family living area, I sensed his anxiety to be gone, and realised we had nothing more to say. I spent the last night on a thin mattress on the floor, my head spinning in a severe relapse of vertigo.

At the appointed hour the following afternoon, I wandered through the empty rooms, a tightness behind my eyes and in my throat, before dropping the keys on the kitchen bench and walking down the hall. My remaining possessions sat in a cubic-metre storage container in a warehouse, and my life boiled down to the contents of the backpack which I heaved onto my shoulders. Stepping out for the last time, I closed the front door firmly behind me. As I walked the bush path to my friends' place, dry leaves crunched under my feet, releasing the tang of eucalyptus.

Some days later, the time came to head back to Arequipa. Rachel, staying with Richard for a few weeks before she set off on a trip overseas, arrived to take me to the airport. She seemed excited and optimistic, and when she dropped me off, I wrapped my arms around her. 'Love you,' I said softly.

'Love you too,' she replied.

I watched her drive away, and headed into the terminal, telling myself, pointlessly, to leave all regrets and nostalgia behind.

CHAPTER 21

The plane touched down in Arequipa mid-afternoon twenty-five hours later. Reaching the tarmac, I put on my dark glasses and scrutinised the terminal, spotting a figure waving from the observation balcony, a slight man in a fetching straw hat. Grinning broadly, I hurried towards him. As I neared the building, a shrill cry rang out.

'Mees Soosi!'

I stopped and looked up. A crowd of youngsters in worn tracksuits and uniforms clustered above me, leaning over the railing, waving hand-painted banners, 'Bienvenida a casa! Welcome home!' and calling out my name. I gasped … Rosa had brought the children of Colegio Elohim to the airport to meet me. As I finally arrived outside with my luggage, they surged forward, and we all tumbled onto the ground, a melée of squeals and kisses. The loss of my home and my scattered family all receded as I hugged every one of them and realised that, for the moment, at least, I had returned to my right place on this Earth.

I went out to the school the following day and stood at the gate before a three-storey building standing out in the dust, amid neighbouring shacks and stone walls. I heard chatter, laughter, scraping chairs, a teacher giving instructions, somewhere a class singing. Once inside, I clambered over thirty kindergarten children who had rushed out into the patio to tackle me round my knees. Upstairs, I found Rosa in her airy office, speaking softly to a nervous young woman in a tracksuit beside a little girl in a faded dress. Slipping out again, I wandered the new classrooms to chat to the teachers and see for myself students busily working at their desks, writing and drawing, or discussing with classmates. The walls were adorned with colourful posters, and shelves for books, backpacks, liquid hand-wash, paper towels, even some toothbrushes and cups. In the toilets, a new experience for most, students scooped water with small buckets from the huge plastic drums to flush, before carefully washing their hands.

Bouncing down the hill in the combi after school I reflected that the benefits of the new building would continue as more classes moved through it on their way, hopefully, to better prospects ahead. I thought of Rosa in her new office. She knew every child, every family, and every domestic situation, offering parents sympathy, and sound counsel; but she didn't take any nonsense, either. Over the years, I'd watched her dish out the same advice over and over again.

'You must make an effort, Gabriella/Katarina/ Josefina, and you know we'll do everything possible to help you! But first, make a start yourself, and stop drinking/use birth control/don't let him beat your children. And no, Gabriella/Katarina/Josefina, you cannot put una niñita aged four all by herself on the combi to ride to school, and then find her way home to wait in the shack, while you stay out working … and no, leaving the seven year old to mind the babies is not the solution! And of course, Gabriella/Katarina/Josefina, if your husband/boyfriend gave up drinking beer/pisco for a week, you could, indeed, pay the enrolment fee of 40 soles ($16) each year, plus the 70 centimos (28 cents) a day for your children's hot lunch at school.'

I coined the name 'Santa Rosa de Arequipa' long ago, for she rarely criticised anyone, despite the behaviours she'd encountered, while I, impatient and judgemental, would have happily strangled some of the parents. Rosa battled to keep children at school against alcoholism, ignorance, suspicion, prejudice, abuse and abandonment. She worked, day after day, late into the nights, on administration, accounts, teaching, counselling, supplies, resources, maintenance, and several times she'd fronted up to the police with serious domestic violence cases. Through it all, she always made time to see the children who frequently arrived at her office, bursting to tell her something important, or just for a cuddle.

She often thanked God in her school prayers for sending me with my 'generous heart'. I felt grateful for the compliment, but more so, that I had found her. When my life floundered in sadness without direction, her faith and vision had turned it around, giving me a purpose, and a way forward.

'Bajo!' someone called out and the combi slowed. I stood to move to the front as it reached my stop.

My! This is different!

With a red and blue jester's hat upon my head, I was running, at a snail's pace, around a circle of chairs while music played from a CD player with a long extension cord leading into the courtyard. It suddenly stopped, and I flapped around until all the small children of Grade 1 had darted to a seat, before crying, 'Oh no! I'm out!' Next I baby-stepped a relay with the four year olds; danced in a competition with Grade 5; wobbled through a potato-and-spoon race with Grade 3; grovelled in the dirt piling up plastic plates with Grade 4; floundered around trying to pop two balloons tied to my ankles by Grade 6; and failed miserably in an attempt to balance a plastic bottle full of water on my head with Grade 2. This year, my fifty-seventh birthday family consisted of the entire population of Colegio Elohim and we were celebrating accordingly.

At the end of the games, Marco and Claudio, twins in Grade 3, showed off an astonishing talent – break dancing! As the reggaetón pounded out of the loudspeaker, they thrilled the entire school with a display of extraordinary rock-hard-headedness, whirling and twirling upside down, right way up and every other which way in between, in a special performance in my honour.

Antonio invited me for a night in a luxury hotel in town to complete the festivities. We had both been busy in our work since my return, and had hardly seen each other, let alone broached any issues about our future. For the moment, I felt content to lie in his arms, remember the events of my birthday, and let my thoughts drift around opposite extremes.

A week later, one of the twins, Claudio, staggered into Colegio Elohim with angry red welts and bruises all over his body, while Marco didn't appear at all. Rosa took the boy straight down the hill to the suburban police headquarters to file a criminal report. The children's mother eventually turned up there, with Marco in tow. He'd taken to the hills that morning when she began thrashing his brother with electric cable wire, apparently because they didn't get up early enough to sweep the dirt floor before going to school.

The local paper reported the incident, the front page wailing, 'She went too far! Mother beats children!' with a photo of the young woman; her rough-burned face set in sullen resentment, sitting on the wall outside the station beside Rosa, watched by two identical, ragged little boys. The twins often hit out and punched other children, but, aged only eight, they still responded to kindness. They lived with their alcoholic single mother, who could remove them from Colegio Elohim at any moment. A few weeks later, furious at the school's role in her brush with the authorities, that's exactly what she did. On the afternoon of the incident, the police had sent her home with her sons and a warning. Once they left Colegio Elohim, the twins no longer had Rosa or the teachers to watch out for them.

I sat at my desk with the birthday cards they'd given me. Each one in an envelope of squared paper, with careful, neat handwriting, 'Feliz Cumpleaños, Miss Susi,' and an intricately cut-out card inside. 'We love you … with hugs on your special day … and Happy Christmas too.' Claudio wrote, 'I wish you could come and visit me,' and Marco's picture had a caption, 'See how I can draw!' I sighed and shook my head. Rosa had done her legal duty in reporting the abuse to the police, but the judicial system hadn't provided the necessary support, sending the two children straight back into the sole control of their destitute mother. Claudio and Marco, basically abandoned, teetered on the brink of a life of crime, and there was not a thing we could do about it.

CHAPTER 22

Just after my birthday, on my way out to Colegio Elohim once more, I waited at the Feria Altiplano marketplace in front of the fruit stalls as usual to change combis.

'Hola, Mees Soosi!' Stephanie from Grade 1 said as she approached, brown eyes lighting up her sweet face, front milk teeth decayed to tiny needles. Her mother arrived, weather-burned features set off by a flat straw hat above her faded tracksuit. She smiled, sporting several large gaps, and I thought of the tooth brushing we tried to instil at school, hoping it wasn't too late for Stephanie. The combi skidded to a stop with horn blasting and the young conductor bundled us on board. We rattled along the wide street past a muddle of buildings with steel conduits sticking out from their roofs, and the occasional courtyard blossoming with colour amid drab cement. In a park, municipal workers in wide-brimmed hats watered the grass from hoses, while others swept the street kerbs, cloth wrapped around their faces against the dust kicked up by their brooms.

Off the asphalt we hit dirt, the combi crawling steadily up and up, bouncing through potholes, all windows now firmly shut. We called to the driver to stop as we spotted students hurrying to jump on, dust swirling in each time the door opened.

Today promised to be special. The year drawing to its close, Grade 5 had organised morning tea to farewell Grade 6. At midday, the hosts invited the guests of honour to take their seats at the table, laden with wafer biscuits, chips, cheese pops and Inca Cola, the intensely sweet national soft drink. Grade 5 began, one by one, to give short speeches of farewell. Several of the leaving girls slumped forward, their heads on the table, and I realised they were crying.

Then came Rosa's turn to speak. She told of her childhood; her mother, born in Cusco, unschooled and desperately poor, her father, a violent drunk. Her home a stone hut. No water, no sanitation. No money for schoolbooks, mockery from other students … until a nun changed her life. Within a year she went from the bottom of the class to the top, and there she stayed. I already knew some of Rosa's background, but I had never heard these details, and I sat bolt upright, my writer's ears twitching, as she ended passionately, 'You can do it, yes you can, no matter how hopeless things may seem. Always, always, God will be there beside you.'

By now, every member of Grade 6 was crying. Many, on leaving Colegio Elohim, would lose the one refuge, the one constant which existed in their troubled lives. Déborah, her face buried in her arms, lived in a shack high up in the hills beside the city garbage dump, where her mother worked collecting recyclable bottles. This woman had doubtless lived through horrors I couldn't even imagine, shaping her life and her reactions to the school. She complained continually, accused Rosa of corruption, seldom participated in anything, and kept her daughter away from classes for days on end. I could only guess at Déborah's home life, but she spent much of her time at school surly and withdrawn, shedding silent tears. Paulo, the tallest boy in the class, nearly a man, who had begun to cry during Rosa's story, burst into sobs afresh as he tried to talk to the class. 'Mi mamá … mi papá …' He spoke of his shame, of his drunken parents, but when his mother Inocencia arrived unexpectedly some time later, his face lit up.

The speeches over, we brought out morning tea and put on some music to lighten the mood. I handed out jackets and sweaters I'd found in cupboards cleaning out my home in Sydney, and watched the children pull them on with beaming smiles and laughter. The decorations which had been part of our Sydney family Christmas for over twenty years now hung from the tree in the classroom.

After the morning tea, I attended Rosa's interview with Paulo's mother about his further education, sitting next to this woman who, to me, appeared at least seventy, but in fact shared my age. She'd had eight children, her oldest thirty-seven and Paulo the youngest at twelve. She could neither read nor write, and her alcoholism had reached the terminal stage – little wonder, but not much help for Paulo. Rosa, trying to arrange secondary studies for him, gently asked if there might be a family member he could board with; but he wanted to stay with his mamá. I reflected on unconditional love.

I had visited their home a year earlier with Rosa, and stood where the gate hung lopsided in the shambling stone wall, staring at a dusty yard full of building rubble and animal droppings. Watching several hens and three mongrels poking around in torn bags bursting full of old rubbish, I'd felt my stomach heave as the smell hit me. Trying to spot an entrance to the shack among hanging rags and shredded plastic, I'd been unable to guess where anyone could have even sat, let alone cooked or slept. I'd felt ashamed of my relief when a neighbour shouted that Inocencia had gone out – so we'd been able to retreat without venturing inside.

The interview over, I rode down in the combi with Paulo and Inocencia and left them at the stop nearest the Municipal Office, knowing I did not have the language to be of any help to them in the face of

Peruvian bureaucracy, and aware that my foreign appearance would more likely have confused matters. I peered through the window at the young boy standing uncertainly with his stooped mother leaning on his arm, clutching her crumpled identity card and a letter from Rosa. With this they would try to register Paulo as legally existent, which hadn't happened when he'd been born. Without this civil status, he could not begin secondary school. Only thanks to Rosa's records from years back, when his mother still remembered the date she'd given birth to her last son, did Paulo have a chance to be recognised as a member of the population of Peru.

How would he manage? I knew acutely how precarious was the line between surviving to become a responsible citizen, and falling into a gang of thugs like those who'd kidnapped Antonio and me. Delinquency hovered, a real and terrifying option for youngsters trying to claw their way out from a mire of brutal poverty and neglect.

December at the institute was always manic, with teachers required to extend all their lessons by ten minutes in order to fit in the required hours before Christmas. Antonio left home early, returned for lunch when I was out at Colegio Elohim, and came back late in the evening, so our paths crossed only for brief, hurried moments; a situation which kept things superficial and, truth be told, peaceful. Nonetheless my mistrust and uncertainty, dormant for months while I was away, soon returned, although once again I could never find concrete proof.

One hot afternoon, the combi ground up to Cenepa, taking me to the final, formal celebration of the Grade 6 graduation. Luz Marina, one of the participants, climbed on in her school tracksuit, her long hair freshly curled and adorned with sparkling sequins. Waving to me, she perched beside a young mother breast-feeding a baby in the front of the combi and began chatting to her. Around them piled the enormous striped plastic sacks in which locals heaved everything from potatoes to toilet paper and fragile eggs, from the market back to their homes in the hills. An elderly woman in a faded dress and thin cardigan, grey hair knotted in a plait, pushed her way through to the back and sank down into the space next to me.

'Es mi hija menor,' she said. At least ten years older than me (I hoped), she'd just announced that eleven-year-old Luz Marina was her youngest; going on to point out the other woman, her oldest, at thirty-eight, and the baby, her granddaughter. I asked her how many children she had. 'Eight,' she said. I calculated in silence – her oldest, born ten years before my first, and her youngest, ten years after my fourth.

The combi reached the college and Luz Marina hurried off down a steep track towards a hut across the road, calling over her shoulder that she was going to change for the ceremony.

The designated starting time, 3 pm, ticked past. Colegio Elohim waited, festooned with green and white silk and balloons, a morning's labour by the teachers. Not a parent, not a student in sight. Ten minutes later, Paulo appeared, alone, in a T-shirt and jeans and my old jacket. His mother had drunk herself into oblivion, so would not be attending.

'It's too late!' Rosa cried. 'The children won't come! All that work, all that preparation, all that food, for nothing! Es un poco difícil!' I put my arm around her, smiling at her favourite understatement, then went to the gate, crossed the dusty street and called out, 'Luz Marina! Where are you?' Moments later she appeared, in pink taffeta, carefully picking her way up the stony path in her new plastic sandals. An ancient car spluttered to the gates, and from it emerged a pretty young vision in white satin, while another, similarly radiant, approached on foot through the dust with her mother. The next combi rolled up the road, stopped at the corner, and out stepped Lucía, in green, flanked by older sister Veronica and mother Pamela. Then came Déborah, looking gorgeous in black which set off her olive skin. She had walked three kilometres across the valley in the fierce afternoon sun with her sister … and her mother had come, too. Another girl hurried in, before two more boys arrived, one wearing jeans and his brother's denim jacket, the other in suit and tie; and the final lad, two hours late.

The ceremony proceeded with speeches, dancing and presentation of framed certificates, the girls smiling in their beauty, the boys awkward but pleased in their formal attire. Today belonged to the children, an afternoon stretching into evening to celebrate achievement, friendship, pride and hope.

CHAPTER 23

Antonio suggested we hold a Christmas Eve celebration at home and I agreed some entertaining would make a pleasant change. We invited Anja and her Bolivian boyfriend, who both arrived at 8.30 pm, and Rosa and her husband, teenage son and adult daughter, who finally rang the bell two hours later, blaming the combi. We wasted no time opening the presents and then began the turkey dinner with potatoes, vegetables and plenty of wine.

Tongues loosened and Anja spoke of the sound of boots crunching through brilliant white snow in the darkness of a Danish Christmas. I reminisced about eating plum pudding in the humid Australian summer and Rosa told us of a dawn pilgrimage she'd made as a child, climbing to a cross on the top of a steep desert hill outside Arequipa. Juan, a chef as well as a teacher, complimented me on the turkey, and helped himself several times to mashed sweet potato and apple sauce, recipes from my dancing girlfriends at the club.

'I carried the bird early this morning down to the bakery oven,' I told them, 'all dressed and ready in its metal dish. I went back four hours later to collect it, but the cooking had released at least two litres of juices. They smelt delicious but they weighed a ton. I carted it back with such pains shooting up and down my back, I had to stop four times and rest. Never again! Next time, I'll cook it at home.'

We finished off the pannetón fruit pastry just in time to stand at the back window and view the whole of Arequipa setting off fireworks at midnight. 'Feliz Navidad', a popular seasonal jingle, burst forth from the radio and we all sang along. Our guests finally left at 1 am to make their way home through noisy crowds who would remain up all night celebrating, to sleep right through the following day.

So often when couples separate, close friends react in shock. 'But, we had dinner with them just a few weeks ago. Everything seemed normal.' My nativity celebration with Antonio did not truly reflect our domestic life, which had been on eggshells since I had returned. Anja, for one, noticed how many times he found pretexts to pop into to his room that festive evening. After alcoholic excesses at two social events in the following week, our life together at Francisco Mostajo hurtled to its sudden and final demise. I asked him to leave, and he readily agreed.

All the same, by the Sunday morning he moved out, nostalgia had once again blurred the unpleasant facts. After two hours spent carting boxes and furniture down the stairs, the moment finally arrived when the loaded van waited ready in the street. As we flung our arms around each other, he murmured, 'I can't live without you.' We both knew in our heads that he couldn't live with me, either … but it didn't make parting any easier on our hearts. The truck headed off. Closing the door to the street, I leaned my back against it, closed my eyes and took a long, deep breath.

Alone in the flat, immediately reverting to frenzied activity to deflect the grief, I began to take apart our life in Francisco Mostajo. Through bathrooms, bedrooms, study and kitchen, I scrubbed, tidied, threw out, re-arranged and de-cluttered. I'd reached a crossroads; whether an end or a beginning, I didn't yet know.

The following day, after a night of steady rain, I turned my attention to the plants. The neighbours' association had decided that due to drainage problems all window gardens had to be replaced by pots. Leaning over the sill in the soggy gloom, I patted out and levelled the damp earth, bare and empty of growth. I remembered the snapdragons, daisies and carnations which had once filled the sunny bed with bright colour, and the bags of garden trimmings I'd hauled upstairs to nourish them. I had just dismantled my old life in Sydney; and now, pressing down the final corners, I realised the same was happening here in Arequipa.

By mid-afternoon, I'd cleaned all the windows and got started on the enormous parquet floor. I swept, washed and spread the wax, then on hands and knees I polished every square centimetre. Two hours later, I got to my feet as a line floated out from a song on the CD, 'If only I could turn back time'. I exhaled and shook my head. No thanks. I'll stay right here in the present. Not for anything would I re-live the last five years; and neither would I ever wax another wooden floor.

Antonio had rented a small house nearby, once again insisting, 'You're still my girl'; and once again, I allowed myself to be persuaded. We settled into a routine of an intimate lunch at his house every Sunday and scant contact during the week as we lived our separate lives. I no longer felt trapped. It should have been perfect. Yet deep down I wondered if the romantic love had suffered too much to salvage, on my part at least. It may take months, it may take years, but was the writing on the wall?

CHAPTER 24

'I remember the day so clearly. I was just a little girl.' Rosa sat opposite me in the back room at Francisco Mostajo. Beyond the window, El Misti loomed, his sombre blue shadows streaked with snow against the grey backdrop of a January morning. Eager for a project, I had asked her to elaborate on her speech at the Grade 6 farewell.

'Under my blanket I felt my hair being pulled gently,' she continued, 'and I wriggled until I finally had to open my eyes. I could just see my mother's shape leaning over me in the dawn, humming softly as she plaited my hair. When she'd finished, I murmured, "Gracias, Mamá," and watched her slide out of our bed like a dark, quiet ghost, without waking Gloria or Ronald. She twisted her hair into a bun, pulled on her jumpers and skirts, thick sandals and the old warm jacket she always wore to her work, where she sorted piles of wool shorn from the alpacas and their cousins the vicuñas. I hated the animal grease which used to cover my hands when I went to help her in the holidays … but today I'd escape because I had to go and collect my annual student report. Usually parents did, but Mamá had to work and as for Papá, whenever he turned up at school drunk and violent, ready to make a scene, I felt so frightened and embarrassed, I just wanted to die.'

She shook her head and grimaced at a memory I couldn't even imagine.

'When I heard her shut the front door quietly, I sat up and groped for the rubber sandals on the wooden box by the bed, pulling them on so my feet wouldn't touch the dirt floor. I crept over to the kerosene stove and found half a cup of oats and a jug of water which Mamá had put out ready for me to cook when the others woke up. My insides grumbled as I thought of the breakfast we'd be sharing that morning. As usual, Mamá had left my apron for me, even though it wasn't a real school day. I peeped into Papá's room but I couldn't see him. He must have stayed out all night again with his friends.

'After getting Gloria and Ronald dressed and serving out hot runny porridge, I left them playing at our kind neighbour's place, and walked to my primary school. I reached the gate and peered round it into the courtyard – Señorita Lelia stood talking to a group of parents from my grade. I swallowed, took a deep breath and walked in. She turned around and saw me, and said loudly, "Ah! Rosa! You've come alone? Your mamá and papá couldn't make it?" She went on to the other adults as if I wasn't even there, "This child lives in a shack in the slums. Her father's a hopeless drunk; her mother works all day and never comes to the school. Her parents can neither read nor write, so she gets no support at home."

'She handed over an envelope and scowled at me. "Your report is not up to standard. You'll have to repeat the year." A lump came into my throat, and I felt hot all over.

'Grabbing it, I ran, without turning around, as fast as I could down the dusty street, and I kept going until I felt sure that no-one could see me. I stopped, puffing so much I could hardly breathe – and tore the envelope open. Out came a stiff paper with a jumble of letters and numbers that made no sense. Sitting in the dust, I covered my face with my dirty hands, and began to cry.'

My chest tightened as, decades later, I shared the abandoned little girl's distress.

'When I'd finally smeared the tears away and stopped them long enough, I set off walking again, till I arrived home ... and found the door unlocked. I started to shake. Papá must have come back. I pushed it open, and crept down the dirt passage to hide my report in the bedroom. Suddenly a tall black figure surged from nowhere, blocking my way. I got such a shock I stumbled backwards and nearly fell over. I sniffed the sour smell Papá always had when he got drunk and angry.

'"Tu libreta!" he boomed, so loud I felt as if he'd boxed my ears. I gulped, and handed it over.

'"What does it say?"

'I just hunched and squeezed my lips tight together, I was so scared.

'He roared even louder, "Tell me!"

'I forced out a squeak, so he wouldn't hit me. "I have to repeat the year."

'He swore horrible words, spit flying from his mouth. Storming out, he stamped back a few seconds later with a thin stick whip which he tapped against his other hand. I remember his face so vividly; wild and wet and twisted, close enough to see his pupils, bulging and shiny; I smelt beer on his breath and the stink of his sweat. Vomit rose in my throat, but I swallowed hard because I knew that would have made him madder.

'"We'll see if this won't loosen the block in your stupid head," he growled, and his hot, clammy hand grabbed the back of my neck.'

Rosa's eyes filled with tears as she relived the moment in my back room overlooking the volcanoes slowly disappearing behind cloud. 'He thrashed me until my knees gave way. When Mamá came home late in the evening she found me huddled in the corner, cut to ribbons, all over my back, my shoulders, legs, head and face. De verdad, that day, I truly believe he wanted to kill me.

'Mamá didn't know I had to go to school when I turned six. With illiterate parents, a mother who worked from dawn till dark and a drunk for a father, of course I lagged behind the others. I started a year late, and I had no idea at all about reading and writing when I finally reached Grade 1. No help or support came from home. None. Nada!

'Some of the others in my class took their cue from the teacher, laughing at me and chanting, "She can't do it!" A girl who lived in a house far away from my shack, said to me one day, "Your papá is a drunk and your mamá is a peasant. You're all dirty *inmigrantes* from the mountains."

'It got to the stage where I felt ashamed walking with my mother. Poor thing, she did everything she could. She always bought me an exercise book or some pencils when she had enough money. I found clean clothes laid out every morning for me to get Gloria and Ronald ready before I went to school. She did her best to leave food, oats or broth from water and animal intestines the butcher sometimes gave her. But some days there'd be nothing, so we began the day hungry, and we stayed hungry, till our growling stomachs made us sick. Sometimes I took little Gloria with me rather than leave her at home with my father.'

She stopped and looked directly across at me.

'Can you believe it? I was seven years old.'
I gazed back. No, I couldn't.

★

One drizzly morning during that January, I headed out to the supermarket off the Avenida Ejercito to buy some supplies. With a group of other pedestrians I stepped off the kerb and we forced the chaotic traffic to stop as we crossed. Rounding the corner, I glanced at two children on the footpath, and did a double take. 'Lucía, Marcelo!' I'd last seen Lucía in a stunning outfit at the graduation ceremony for Grade 6 at Colegio Elohim a month before, accompanied by her mother Pamela. Now she appeared in worn jeans and jumper wearing a special blue apron and holding out a mobile to passers-by who may need to make a call. This job, as a sort of ambulatory telephone, ranks with that of combi conductor as the bottom of the barrel, and, most people owning their own cell phone, she'd be lucky to earn 100 soles ($30) a month. Marcelo, just out of Grade 1 at Elohim, had come along too; caked in grime, bedraggled, painfully thin and ravenously hungry. For the months of January and February, with no school to keep them off the streets, that's exactly where these two had ended up.

Knowing of the family's living conditions, I realised the importance to Pamela of any money her children could earn during the holidays. I also knew, as did she, that both Lucía and Marcelo could have gone to Colegio Elohim for vacation classes and a substantial free lunch. Perhaps Pamela considered sending her daughter and son out to work as responsible behaviour, rather than accepting hand-outs.

I told them to wait while I hurried to the supermarket and returned with ham, cheese, rolls, and two drinks. They ate it all, sitting with me on the dirty footpath while the midday crowd stepped around us. As Marcelo stuffed the food into his mouth, I tried not to think of the germs on his hands which went in with it.

A few days later, in almost exactly the same spot, I ran into Pamela herself, strolling Ejercito with Veronica, her oldest, who'd recently completed her second year in high school. 'Aye, Mees Soosi,' Pamela exclaimed, 'I feel so tired – I deserve some time to relax, away from my children, don't you agree?' Remembering my early days as a privileged young mother of (only) four, I had to concede that she had a point. I later discovered that, on the same day, while she was out, her third daughter, nine-year-old Sofía, had arrived in the combi at Elohim for lunch; bent under the weight of Hugo, the latest baby, slumbering in a blanket on her back, and leading three-year-old Rafael by the hand.

★

I understood the reality Rosa had grown up with when she invited me to the family home where her parents still lived along with her two nephews and her sister Gloria. As the combi rattled down paved streets, past churches, schools and parks, I guessed that the physical environment had much improved since Rosa's childhood. Approaching the house from the street, we noticed two drunks sitting on a step nearby. 'Friends of mi papá,' said Rosa, opening the front door to an uncovered corridor. We walked past a modern kitchen, bathroom and two bedrooms on the left, and on the right, Rosa pointed to her father's room, still with dirt floor, old iron bed and table fashioned from a tree stump. Reaching an unpaved courtyard, strung with clothes lines, we crossed in front of a small toilet cubicle, to enter another bedroom, cluttered and smelling like a second-hand clothes shop with a strong tang of urine. Crumpled garments lay all over the place, covering two beds and shelves leaning on stained, damp walls. In the middle of one mattress huddled Rosa's mother, Alvina.

Eighty years of toil and sorrow had taken their toll. Cusco bowler hat upon two thin grey plaits, she crouched and shivered despite thick stockings, socks, skirts and a knitted shawl. Her filmy eyes could barely focus; her toothless mouth, hardly utter a word.

Greeting her with a hug, I feared her skeletal shoulders would crack. She stared at the bunch of flowers I gave her, mumbled something, then plucked a daisy and put it into her mouth. She sat chewing it as we quietly left the room.

I didn't know what to expect of Rosa's father, whose addiction had caused his family so much suffering. Statistics would have predicted his death along with his alcoholic contemporaries many years before, but somehow he'd survived to reach the age of seventy. He finally appeared, a small, wiry man with jet-black hair and dark eyes, hurrying over to us, talking excitedly through several missing teeth. I heard *gringas* and *visitas* and I'm not sure what else. He burst into song with an old lament in the indigenous Quechua language and for the next half hour he regaled us with what I gathered were tales from his childhood. We ate a lunch of pork, prepared by Gloria, also a dedicated teacher, working full-time and raising her sons alone.

It might have been a normal family meal with an eccentric but amusing old papá and his daughters … until the young girl who cared for Alvina came to help clear the table and made a remark about the individuals drinking at the front door. Without warning, the old man jumped up with clenched fists raised, letting fly with a tirade of fury and foul language, before charging from the room. Watching him, I thought of seven-year-old Rosa facing a much younger, stronger parent with her school report. Moments later, he stormed outside carrying his rumpled old coat.

'He's gone,' said Gloria sadly, 'to get drunk with his new young friends.'

I didn't see him again.

Lying in bed that night, the scene still churning in my head, I pictured him coming home in an incoherent rage, yelling, shoving at his poor, spent wife as he apparently continued to do after a lifetime abusing her. His five-year-old grandson, screaming at him, trying to protect frail, confused Alvina. Gloria, sickened as she watched her younger boy stand up to the insane raving of his grandfather. Her older son attempting to remain aloof from it all as befits a cool, modern teenager who tried to laugh off his grandfather's ranting aggression, telling me it was 'odd'. At least they lived comfortably in a modern wing of the house. I shut out thoughts of what alcohol-fuelled cruelty might go on behind the walls of some of those dirt-floored shacks up there in Héroes del Cenepa.

When Alvina finally gave up on life and slipped away two years later, I could only hug Rosa and agree that, at last, her mother was at peace.

CHAPTER 25

A fortunate encounter delivered me a buyer for 301/808 Francisco Mostajo. I emptied the flat, sold everything, even Esmerelda the washing machine, to keen middle-class bargain hunters who beat me down to the last centavo, and relocated to rent a tiny partly-furnished cottage around the corner. 'Rustic' would have been the word used by a Sydney real estate agent. A match-lit gas contraption delivered hot water for my shower, the toilet cistern leaked constantly, I cooked on a gas ring, the floor tiles were cracked and the worn carpet had a huge hole in it. But the living and sleeping area was elevated, with sliding glass panes through which poured the afternoon sun as it rapidly dried hand-washed clothes strung on the miniscule balcony. The generously-sized bedroom had ample space for my writing table with a view over the garden; and when I stood in the kitchen I felt as if I lived in a treehouse amid the jacaranda branches, watching through the open window as tiny colourful birds flitted less than a metre in front of me among the leaves in dappled sunlight. In this garden paradise I finally returned to a life unencumbered by domestic clutter. Soon after, Antonio established himself in his own apartment, living above his ex-wife on the top floor of the family home.

My cottage lay separated from the noise of the street by trees, grass and a high wall with a secure locked gate. Most mornings I roamed the cobbled laneways of Yanahuara, passing the milkman pushing his cart with bicycle wheels, bumping along the cobbles balancing large metal urns of warm creamy liquid. I'd buy *La Republica* from the barrow of the bellowing newspaper lady surrounded by her côterie of scruffy strays, before greeting the elderly man sitting on the kerb beside boxes of avocadoes, tomatoes and mangoes, where I always purchased a kilo of sweet figs. Sometimes a señora would pass by, wheeling a trolley bag of hot baked stuffed potatoes which smelt like stew, as she called out 'papas rellenas!' One day, a beautiful young woman walked towards me carrying a wicker basket filled with jars of honey. She wore the full skirts, stockings and traditional blouse and jacket of the Andes, complete with a gurgling baby on her back. Another neighbourhood regular, the man with his cart full of green alfalfa, regularly parked it on a corner, handing out bundles to his customers. I knew they fed it to their guinea pigs … pets sentenced to be cooked over a fire and served spread-eagled on a plate, including the head.

A laneway took me past a local restaurant, where the door often flew open, spilling out several young chefs in white caps, red-faced and straining under giant metal dishes held high, groaning with trays of uncooked potato bake and pork. They'd puff past over the cobbles and around the corner, bearing the day's menu two blocks down the road to the oven.

By now I was dancing in the evenings as well, and on the way home from the class I always stopped at the local store which sold everything from avocadoes to super glue. Here I could shop on a small scale … a cup of laundry detergent, three eggs in a plastic bag, a sachet of shampoo, two or three teabags, two Panadol, a handful of peppercorns. I had learned patience with other customers who invariably began calling their orders as soon as they walked in the door, unconcerned whether the friendly shopkeeper was already serving someone else. He would simply break off from serving me to respond to every new arrival. Long before, when I had first vented to Antonio about the rudeness of Arequipeñans, he had explained to me the owner's economic necessity not to turn anyone away. These small commerces, called *bodegas*, abound on every street corner, offering plenty of choice to any dissatisfied customer, so it is firmly in the shopkeeper's interests to keep everyone content. Now, I simply admired how he could engage with four of us at once, darting here and there fetching for everyone, not once becoming flustered or impatient ... such a contrast to the regimented queues in government departments, banks and telephone offices, where customers waited patiently for their number to be called, while an armed security guard hovered nearby.

On occasions I'd hear the sound of a tuning whistle and grab my kitchen knife to race out and catch the blade sharpener. He always charged me three soles, about $1.20, to tip his cart upside down, spin its wheel and turn the razor strap, sparks flying as he ground my domestic implement into a potentially deadly weapon. Some evenings, I listened to the African Peruvian sitting astride his box drum beneath the street lamp, selling chicken or meat cornmeal. His fingers flicking against the wood conjured up dark jungle images as he chanted, 'Tamales! Tamales!' in a performance always worth one of his steaming delicacies wrapped in a banana leaf. Every morning and evening, the smell of bread just out of the oven wafted out from the bakery, meaning a detour through the door for a cheese or spinach pastry empanada ... and, when my willpower evaporated, a chunk of warm yellow corn cake.

Opening the high gate and hearing it click behind me, I'd enter my garden domain. Hummingbirds hovered and whirred over the honeysuckle in the morning sunshine, yellow roses loaded the afternoons with their sweetness, and at night, the moon tracked its cycle across the sky, from thin crescent to round ball.

In my 'rustic' home, I prepared food as I wanted … fresh salads and local fruits, rinsed thoroughly in boiled water with drops of bleach added; lightly steamed vegetables, toasted pan de trigo with butter and Vegemite, local round yellow tilsit cheese, boiled eggs, and simply cooked chicken, meat and fish. Heaven.

One afternoon, standing at the open kitchen window, I watched a tiny hummingbird hovering among the jacaranda blooms. It came closer, its feathers gleaming greeny-turquoise in the sun between the branches as its wings quivered silently, so fast they didn't seem to be moving at all. I could have tickled its lilac chest with my finger, but as if guessing my thoughts, it suddenly dropped, hung suspended below me a moment, then whirred out and away into the blue sky.

A crackling screech shattered the peace, a lusty female voice yodelling out the theme from the movie *Titanic*; 'Near, … faaaar, … Wher-eeee-ver yo-u aaaare …', the signal for people to bring out their bulging and odorous plastic bags as the local garbage truck revved and ground its gears, blasting its way down the narrow road beyond my hidden garden. The municipality did not provide rubbish bins because they would immediately disappear, and although streetside notices threatened fines for refuse left out more than ten minutes before collection time, working residents skirted this problem by leaving it on deserted street corners early in the mornings, to fester anonymously at the mercy of stray animals until the afternoon pick-up. The signs were about as effective as the four which had been stuck into the grass all over the Plaza Yanahuara, cute Labrador puppies bearing a message that their poops were their owners' responsibility, but with no accompanying roll of plastic bags or bin in sight; or the monstrous placards erected by the committee at the club reminding us about the environmental danger of traffic fumes, with no apparent awareness of the issue of visual pollution.

As the ancient sanitary vehicle advanced over the cobbles, the neighbourhood dogs started up their hysterical barking, enraged by the loud music, the smell, and the engine noise. I couldn't see them, but I knew they were hurtling around their flat cement rooftops, stopping dead at the edge, teetering as they peered down at the trundling invader, not daring to launch themselves several storeys into the street.

It occurred to me that, with more choices than these canine prisoners, long ago I did indeed steel my nerve and take off … as fast, and as far away, as possible. Finally coming to rest here, in a town in the desert foothills of the Andes.

★

In early March, the night before the start of the school year, Rosa's phone rang at 10 pm, just as she had finished her final preparations and was heading to bed.

'I'm in Arequipa with a group of volunteer dentists from the States, and they're ready to work at the clinic tomorrow,' announced a strident male voice attempting castellano over the phone. 'Send over some children who need attention!'

It was Jimmy, visiting from the US.

At 10.30 pm Rosa rang me to explain that she wouldn't be at school the next day as she'd be taking some pupils across town to the dental clinic. When she told me the circumstances, steam shot out of my ears. Who the heck did this person think he was? Ringing the school director late on the evening before the academic year began, expecting her to drop everything and traipse across town in a taxi because he'd summoned her? Rosa had agreed, as always, for the sake of the children.

'I'll come too,' I said innocently.

The following morning, accompanied by four little students with toothache, we arrived in a taxi at the gate of a painted brick house behind iron grillwork and, inside the door, entered a fresh, modern surgery. Jimmy, a rotund, balding man in his sixties rushed up to greet us, then proudly showed us the waiting room, two dental chairs, various drills and equipment, plus hundreds of toothpaste and toothbrush samples.

Two American dentists, a young woman and a middle-aged man, began working with the children, while Jimmy snapped photo after photo. On the pretext of finding the toilet, I escaped into the house for a quiet scout around. Over three storeys, I discovered a modern kitchen with every imaginable appliance, several bathrooms and four generously-proportioned bedrooms; plus an entire extra wing on the other side of the patio and garden. A very impressive establishment for a low-income suburb. I began to feel uneasy. This luxurious clinic with equally luxurious house attached had no other patients during our visit except the – poor and extremely photogenic – children of Colegio Elohim. Jimmy's snaps of the volunteers attending to them would pull at heart and purse strings in the US, to generate support … and just where exactly would the money end up?

As we were leaving, the older dentist took me aside and asked if we could meet in private. Intrigued, I agreed. Over lunch in town, I had a frank and illuminating conversation with this committed Christian who had spent much of his life working in health missions in the poorest countries of Central America. We decided to test whether tax-deductible donations made in the US to Jimmy for Colegio Elohim were, in fact, getting through. As soon as he returned home, the dentist made a donation of $1000 to the dental clinic, specifying that it go to the school. More than ten weeks later, the transfer still had not reached us. Meanwhile, by asking more questions, I'd found out that the money Rosa had to beg for earlier on for her teachers had not come from Jimmy himself, as I had assumed. A generous doctor in the US had been making regular monthly donations to the clinic, specifically and exclusively for Elohim's staff salaries.

Alarm bells ringing and with Rosa, Sylvia and Yulissa's approval, I wrote a letter in Spanish and English to the dental clinic, disassociating Colegio Elohim from all its activities, and prohibiting Jimmy, or any member of his family, from setting foot inside the school.

We emailed the letter on a Thursday early in May, and the following Sunday, in the middle of her morning church service, Rosa received a call on her mobile.

'Come outside immediately!' Jimmy's Peruvian brother-in-law shouted down the line. She obliged, and found him in his Sunday best pacing up and down with an envelope and a receipt book. 'A donation has just arrived for your school and you must sign and date this official receipt, right now!' he blustered. Noticing it was for only $500, Rosa wrote her name in the required spot. He grabbed it, shoving an envelope into her hands, and rushed to his four-wheel drive, roaring off to his own religious devotions in a cloud of dust.

We never found out what happened to the rest of the money, nor did we hear from Jimmy or his extended Peruvian family ever again.

Thinking of the groups Jimmy had brought to the school in the past, and Rosa's inability to communicate with them, I drafted a strict set of rules for all future visitors. As elsewhere in the world, Peru had been rocked by its share of scandals, and the authorities were becoming more aware of the need to legally protect children. My protocol, in both castellano and English, became school policy.

CHAPTER 26

I wasn't sure if I felt anger, or bitter amusement. We had hired a new legal representative, Dr Nuñez, to examine the constitution of the Asociación Vida y Esperanza through which Rosa ran Colegio Elohim. At our first meeting, he was revealing some hard truths about the church-going-and-acting-for-gringo-missionaries local lawyer who'd set it up. No doubt assuming that Rosa's association would receive substantial handouts from overseas, this gentleman had inscribed no other than … himself … in the constitution as its representing authority, in other words, its owner, and heir to all its assets. He'd hidden this cleverly in several paragraphs of Spanish legalese, and Rosa, Sylvia and Yulissa had never suspected a thing. I glanced over to see them sitting, dumbfounded, listening as Dr Nuñez explained what had been done.

It took him more than a year to sort it out, rewrite the constitution and establish a new board, which

included me. He added a clause that if the association ever wound up, all its assets would go to another
Peruvian benevolent organisation with similar objec-
tives – and not to us.

'Estimado Señor,' began my letter, destined for the
Head Librarian at Arequipa's National Library. My
castellano now up to the task, with a lot of help from
Google Translator, I'd decided to start writing to local
organisations, seeking support for Colegio Elohim.
Formal letters, called *oficios*, are required for any sort
of communication with an educational, government
or commercial institution; and they must be hand-
delivered, in duplicate, with a copy of the sender's
identification document.

The librarian replied at once and welcomed Grades
5 and 6 to the historic building, a converted colonial
Spanish stone villa in the centre of town. Our children
from the outskirts wandered open-mouthed through
the courtyard with its fountain, and on to the reading
lounge lined with bookshelves. A frenzy of hands–on
activities followed in the computer room, until finally,
the staff waved us farewell, no doubt collapsing in
exhaustion once we rounded the corner out of sight.

My next request for assistance involved a trek by
taxi, which I rang from home and, as always, sat in the

front, the friendly driver depositing me at the palatial offices of an international mining company. Hearing of its eagerness to help local causes, given the profits it extracted from the region, I'd put many hours into an oficio setting out a three-year plan and budget, in Spanish, for extensive IT equipment.

The armed guard at the gate took my ID, directing me over manicured lawns to the entrance of a modern open-plan workspace. Here, smartly-dressed locals sat on ergonomic swivel chairs at polished desks before flat computer screens. I was eventually ushered into the private office of the Arequipeñan in charge of local humanitarian projects. After a cordial discussion, I left him with my proposal, hopeful that the company would begin by funding twenty new computers, and continue with more support over the following years.

I rang his long-suffering secretary every week and sometimes every day in my gringa-accented castellano from my crackly mobile. Six months later, I finally heard her announce down the line, 'The Company has agreed to donate computers. I have just sent an email with the details.' My exhilarated dance across the room came to a sudden halt as I reached my screen and began reading. The next week, two ancient, ill-running horrors arrived at the school, so heavy only Juan, at risk of a hernia, could haul them up the stairs. We disposed of them within twelve months, when we acquired twenty brand-new, sleek machines – paid for by donations from generous individuals in Australia and the US.

Undaunted, I continued, with oficios to two universities asking if they could assign us students needing practical experience to help our teachers. Arriving in the combi at the education faculty of the national university, I found reception firmly locked, corridors deserted. The administration section was in the middle of one of its frequent strikes, its battles with government over conditions and salaries so endemic that students always added one extra year to their estimated course lengths, to take account of time lost. I knocked boldly on a door and interrupted a lecture, begging pardon and leaving my document with the somewhat surprised academic staff member. I squeezed her hand, thanked her and left, hoping that it would eventually reach its destination. It didn't, although the following year, I finally met the Dean, who sent three Education students to work with us. Things in Peru happen in their own sweet time … entirely, as I had to once again accept, beyond my control.

I returned to Sydney in December to catch up with Katy, single and much more settled, and Peter. Back from London, he was struggling with devastation having just separated from his bride of fifteen months.

Both Lisa and Rachel had been overseas for some time. On Christmas Day, Peter drove Katy and me to my brother's place for a warmly relaxed family morning.

'Just drop me off at a station, I can get home from there,' I said on the way back at around 1 pm; so Peter did, and continued on with Katy to their grandmother's where they'd been invited for lunch with Richard, his wife and his siblings. As I sat alone waiting for the train, I thought of past nativity turkeys I'd roasted and served out to hungry hordes amid exploding crackers, silly hats, presents and laughter. In the silence of the deserted platform, I heard King Théoden's words from *Lord of the Rings*. 'How did it come to this?'

CHAPTER 27

Upon my return to Arequipa in January, the wet season in full swing, I rushed straight back to dance with Emilio in the cloudy mornings and in the evenings after the inevitable storms, splashing down streets running with rivers of dirty water to get there. On my first weekend, I went to Antonio's apartment for lunch, beginning with a grand tour of the decorations and improvements he'd made. He had created a mix of traditional ochre pottery and woven textiles with greenery and feature walls, one burnished red with a decorative iron window grill at its centre, and the other dusky yellow, with framed sepia photos of historical Arequipa. We both laughed as he pointed out the hated easy chair surrounded by pot plants on his cosy reading patio. As he bustled round his small kitchen preparing fish smothered with tomato and onions and a sauce which really did smell wonderful, I listened eagerly to his animated accounts of all the news I'd missed. Somehow I felt more comfortable as a guest at his home, rather than the other way around, which had been the case when we had lived together in Francisco Mostajo. At around 4 pm, I left him to spend his evening alone.

My cottage, not so idyllic in the wet season, sprang several serious leaks, and afternoon downpours sent water streaming onto my bed, all over the bathroom floor, and into the kitchen to short-circuit the light. Fortunately, my little house had a dry bottom storey, where I moved my mattress, sheets and blankets; I put anything not waterproof into cupboards, and leaving home I'd cover electric appliances and plugs just in case it bucketed during my absence. The landlady organised plastic roof sheeting which helped, and I realised I wasn't the only one with leakage problems when I saw a man belting with a hammer at the brick wall of his house from outside near the pavement level. As soon as he broke through, a flood came gushing out from his living room into the street through the fist-size hole he'd created. By April when neither the cottage roof nor the aperture in my neighbour's exterior wall had been permanently fixed, I told Antonio. 'Why worry about leaks and breaches?' he asked. 'It won't rain again until December!'

When he began complaining about his cable TV reception, I asked him if he'd rung the provider to send out a technician.

'But no, I can't. The network isn't in my name, I share it,' he replied.

The widespread Peruvian attitude is that hoodwinking the authorities, or in this case, the telco, is the only course of action open to any self-respecting citizen, and Antonio had hooked up a connection to feed off his ex-wife's downstairs. She was already sharing with the house next door, so they could split the bill three ways. I had come across this practice in my first flat when the neighbour had offered me access to her internet service if I wanted to drill a hole in the wall and feed a wire through. Not entirely understanding, I had politely refused and organised my own.

Antonio had laughed when I'd mentioned it. 'Ah, yes. In most buildings there is one legal contract, with twenty illegal connections,' adding rather proudly, 'it saves a fortune on bills.'

Soon afterwards he found out that the house next door which shared his cable had no fewer than five televisions … and in a complete about-turn, he organised his own, legitimate, private service.

As my friendships deepened with my dance and meditation companions, I was discovering a group of dynamic, intelligent women at various stages of domestic and professional life. Most had at least one family member living overseas whom they visited regularly; sons and daughters working and raising families with their non-Peruvian spouses in the US, Europe and Scandinavia; or studying at foreign universities in foreign tongues. One, an older friend's brother, was a renowned pianist in Vienna who returned to Arequipa each year for a concert season. Talking to the younger women I found out that one or other child was off on exchange to US, Germany or France to improve their second language, standard practice in the exclusive private schools of the city.

I contemplated the vastly different future prospects facing our pupils in Héroes del Cenepa, and the enormity of the project I had undertaken loomed large.

'Mees Soosi! Pamela's been poisoned! And two of the children! They've been rushed to hospital!'

'I'm on my way. I'll meet you in the Feria in thirty minutes and we can go together by taxi from there.'

In the car, Rosa filled in the details. 'They swallowed insecticide and she's under suspicion for attempted murder-suicide.' We were headed for the Hospital General, the destination for Peruvian patients in extreme poverty, unemployed and therefore without work-related medical insurance. Fearing something out of a Dickens novel, I surveyed a spacious reception area and wide corridors of gleaming linoleum, as a uniformed nurse directed us to the children's wing.

Following shrieks of distress, we rushed into a room where Pamela's youngest, fifteen-month-old Hugo, screamed in a metal cot, skin blotched red, black hair plastered to his head with sweat. We wheeled him out and up the corridor to search for Veronica, hoping that being near his older sister may calm him. We found her in a bed in a shared ward, face pale and drawn, her dark eyes filling with tears when she saw us. She took her baby brother in her arms and nestled her face into his neck, stopping his tears immediately. He sucked his thumb and promptly fell asleep.

'What happened?' Rosa asked gently.

'I drank soft drink out of a bottle open on the table and then started to feel sick,' she murmured, 'Mamá drank some too, and gave Hugo some sips ...' Beside her, a newspaper lay open, headlines screaming, 'Mother tries to kill herself and her children!' with graphic photos of the inside of their hovel and the chaotic yard.

'Who put the bottle there?' asked Rosa.

Veronica looked at her. 'It was an accident.'

We eventually left her, promising to bring back some pyjamas from the market, and headed upstairs where we found Pamela lying back beneath pregnancy number seven due the following week. 'The doctors and the nurses keep asking me why I did it,' she stammered tearfully, 'but, I didn't do anything. One of the kids bought some pesticide and put it in a half-full bottle of lemonade to set a trap for the flies.'

I stared at her enormous belly, thinking about shop-keepers selling poisonous powders in easy-to-open packets to small children; about the legal precept of being innocent until proven guilty, especially if you happen to be a '*chola*', 'Indian', from the slums; about the swarms of black, sticky flies infesting Pamela's place in the wet season; and about the brand new baby who'd soon be taken home to begin life there.

A few days later, Veronica had recovered enough to return to the shack, where she found the police in the yard, dragging out her four younger siblings with jackets over their heads to protect them from flashing cameras. The local press had got wind of the removal of the children and reporters had rushed to the scene for a follow-up to the poisoning story. Veronica crouched behind a wall until they'd all left, and remained alone in the hut until Pamela, still under suspicion, returned a week later with Hugo and her seventh baby, a perfect little girl named Karina.

The four children taken away by the authorities ended up in a private refuge in a pleasant green rural area on the outskirts of town. Rosa and I visited and found them transformed, with sweet-smelling skin, washed and perfumed hair, fresh hand-me-down clothes, plenty to eat, and clean beds to sleep in. They seemed to be interacting with the others happily enough and they all started school at the college next door to the hostel.

'If we pay to help Pamela improve the shack,' I said, 'she's just as likely to use the money for something else. Particularly since her husband is in the background.'

'Gossip would fly about,' warned Rosa, 'probably fuelled by Pamela herself, telling everyone, "The gringa helped me." No, the only thing we can do is offer her some work. Cleaning perhaps.'

'She wouldn't have any idea how to clean a bathroom or a kitchen, never having had one,' I said with a sigh, 'let alone a classroom.'

We decided to offer her some regular paid hours scrubbing pots and pans. She came to school every day, leading Hugo by the hand with baby Karina tied in a blanket on her back. She occasionally upset the other women in the kitchen, refusing to do certain tasks, taking time to attend to her children, or just to sit down and relax; but in her own way, she scoured and polished with impressive persistence. As part of her payment, she took home cooked food for herself plus Veronica and Hugo; and any spare cash she used to buy building materials, week by week.

Pamela told us that when she visited Lucía, Sofía, Marcelo and Rafael at the refuge, they cried and begged to be taken home. She even claimed that her sons had suffered abuse at the hands of the older boys.

'It's certainly possible,' said Rosa. 'The refuges are notorious here in Peru, even the private ones run by churches.'

'But we saw them … clean, eating regular meals, and the carers seem compassionate and kind,' I said.

'Children never lie in things that matter,' she replied quietly, 'and Pamela says they told her.'

I suddenly felt rather unsure, and ashamed of myself.

Over four months, Pamela and her estranged husband put on a front as a united struggling family to convince the social worker, until the refuge returned the children to the hovel. Throughout the second half of the year, we watched them revert to a state of extreme neglect, all eating their main daily meal at Colegio Elohim, except the breastfed baby. Even Lucía and Veronica travelled up for lunch after the morning session at their secondary school, in return for some help organising plates in the kitchen.

Although absent, Pamela's husband made regular financial contributions until they finally completed the roof of a simple two-roomed structure, missing only a door and windows. In November, to ensure shelter from the fast-approaching wet season, we advanced

Pamela the money for these, to be paid for by extra cleaning work the following January.

She didn't show up to complete the hours required to earn the money she'd been given. The children told us their father was paying overnight visits much more often – in far greater comfort now the shack had two rooms instead of just one. Despite twelve months' encouragement and reminders, Pamela still hadn't gone to the local hospital to have her tubes tied, an operation which would cost her nothing.

'Someone told her it may cause cancer,' Rosa said.

'The only death she needs to worry about,' I muttered, 'will be when Miss Susi wrings her neck.'

Several months later she came to Rosa announcing the idea of putting the new, improved shack up as a guarantee, to take out a loan for a business venture suggested by her husband. At the same time, Lucía, employed minding Rosa's two-year-old grandson, helped herself to the best of his young mother's clothes and disappeared. Then Veronica, aged just fifteen and still at secondary school, started going out with a combi driver whom she met on the job while working as a conductor – much older and also married.

'Perfect,' I moaned to Rosa, 'and of course she carries condoms with her, and of course he consents to wearing them.'

We didn't have to be clairvoyant to see what was coming.

CHAPTER 28

Antonio and I continued the routine of having Sunday lunch at his apartment. We still danced together to the radio and our easy conversations would range through the week's local gossip, work, particularly the social and cultural issues thrown up by the struggles at Colegio Elohim; friends, family, national news and insights, and, best of all, books. With his love and extensive knowledge of Peruvian and South American authors, he guided my own efforts with literature in castellano, leading me to discover another world of reading. My first effort, *Aunt Julia and the Scriptwriter*, by Vargas Llosa, native of Arequipa and winner of the Nobel Prize for Literature in 2010, had taken me so long with my dictionary that by the time I'd reached the end, I had forgotten the beginning. Nonetheless I persevered, and managed *The Dream of the Celt*, before moving on to other Peruvian, Colombian and Mexican writers, finally becoming as passionately entwined as Antonio in their plots, their settings, and the sheer beauty of the language and writing style.

But I would always leave his place by 4 pm.

★

Soon after rushing to the Hospital General for Pamela and her children, we did it again for Carolina, our kitchen chef, who landed there fighting for her life after an illegal abortion. I knew she had injections for birth control, but they must have failed. We raced through the crowded reception area and upstairs to the operating rooms, managing to grab a few moments to hold her hands as they wheeled her in, weeping, jaundiced and swollen from serious infection. Next, we darted across six lanes of traffic to the pharmacy to buy all the medications necessary for the treatment, the usual procedure in many Peruvian hospitals.

By mid-afternoon, after six hours waiting for various busy doctors and another fleeting glimpse of Carolina, we both had to leave. On the way out, we ran into her husband who'd finally arrived. We told him we had paid for the medicines and gave him the accounts, suggesting that it was his responsibility to reimburse us … which he never did.

Carolina recovered and returned, weak and worn, to work in the kitchen. Less than four months later, her stomach began to swell visibly – she must have conceived within weeks of the abortion and its terrifying aftermath. She gave birth to her fourth child, a healthy son, the following March. We insisted that if she wished to continue working, he had to be minded at the nearby crèche for 1.50 soles – 60 cents per day. Over time she became progressively thinner and the baby spent less hours in care and more in a blanket on her back while she stirred and hefted the huge, boiling pots.

By October I had to say something. 'Carolina, why isn't your baby at the crèche?'

'I can't afford it,' she whimpered. 'There isn't enough money left from my salary after my husband has made his payment for the car and his driving lessons.'

I swallowed.

'He has failed his licence test three times but when I complain, he shouts at me that he will keep trying until he can become a taxista.'

I told Rosa, who simply shrugged. 'Her husband is a man without shame. Until she leaves him we can do nothing more for her.' A few weeks before, he'd arrived home at midnight in a drunken rage and dragged his two little sons out of bed to watch him beat up an innocent neighbour in an unprovoked attack.

'What can I do for her and those poor children?' I wailed to my friend, a ninety-year-old nun who'd spent sixty years supporting women working as prostitutes in Lima.

She shook her head sadly. 'Susi, we are fighting a whole culture.'

Mulling over her words, I checked the dictionary for machismo and found several definitions. According to one, Latin American males view themselves as conquistadores of women, while females accept a submissive role, and in extreme cases, expect their mates to be aggressive; attitudes I had already recognised in the steps and costumes of the traditional saya dance, to give but one cultural example. Additional theories stated that respect and reverence of the female form and function are integral parts of the machismo culture ... but I suspected that Carolina's husband hadn't heard those.

The mixed messages of TV advertising came to mind ... the dermatologist in her laundry in discussion with her bossy mother about the cleaning agent she uses which protects her hands; or the accountant, praising the soap powder which removes stains from her husband's shirts and little son's football tops; not to mention the father and teenage boys sitting up to a hearty pasta dish served up by their doting mother, helped by her daughter. I remembered my classes at the institute, full of mainly young women, all at university studying to be professionals; and the eight girls I'd known over the years whose unplanned pregnancies had interrupted their tertiary studies ... when every local health centre had the pill available. A young middle-class friend told me that me no-one asks for it, some for traditional

religious scruples, but many for fear of appearing pro-
miscuous; and that even educated men refuse to use
condoms. I thought of my two friends from dance class
who were raising grandchildren in their homes while
their single daughters continued their studies. The
machismo extended as far as middle-class dog owners
who refused to de-sex their animals as it was not natural … more than once in the streets of Yanahuara tes-
tosterone-crazed dogs had chased me as they crowded,
snapping and snarling, outside the gate of a bitch on
heat.

'What a muddle,' I said to myself with a sigh.
'Perhaps it will all change in the next generation, after
mothers have warned their daughters.'

Meanwhile, in the slum of Héroes del Cenepa,
Carolina's oldest, Helena, was growing up followed by
three brothers. At least she'd had eight formative years
at Colegio Elohim, but home was a male-dominated
situation of abuse and poverty. What would be her
expectations from life, having watched the interplay
between her violently alcoholic father and her fiery,
battling mother?

Carolina and Pamela, and the unexpected results
of our attempts to help them, brought to mind the
thorny issue of giving unconditionally, but wisely.
Rosa and I reached a decision. We had to accept
that we could not change the habitual behaviour of
the parents, but we'd do everything in our power

to save the children by pouring all our energies and resources into the school, and only the school. No more attempts to help individual families, no more loans, no more jobs given out of charity.

I had registered Colegio Elohim with Global Development Group, an Australian not-for-profit which assured adherence to Australian government guidelines, and tax deductibility for donations. The name of our project was 'Empowerment through Education' – and from now on this, and only this, would be our vision.

CHAPTER 29

The school marching competition, held in July, was a highlight in the life of one of our most forsaken children. I'd first met Fermín at Colegio Elohim when he was in Grade 2. He lived with his mother and alcoholic stepfather and two younger siblings in a shack in the desolate, dangerous hills above Héroes del Cenepa. He and his younger brother Alfredo had learning difficulties, not helped by the days of school they seemed to miss every week. Fermín also suffered from a severe squint.

When Fermín reached Grade 4, the teachers discovered his natural talent for marching. Selected for the team, he strode with his companions in formation up and down back streets in the hot sun to the beat of a stick on a petrol can; head high, arms swinging. They competed locally before the municipal judges and, to everyone's amazement, got to second place. Then came the district level, which they won.

The day arrived for the final competition, pitting our students against the whole southern area of Arequipa. Arriving at school at 7 am, I watched small figures mincing down dusty paths from their homes in the hills, trying to keep clean long enough to reach the buses which would take us to the parade. Turned out in spotless, pressed white shirts, uniforms, combed and braided hair and shoes shined to mirrors, every child was testimony to extreme effort in conditions which would have reduced me to a tantrum. Clutching the new uniform we'd purchased especially for Fermín, I scoured the desert hills. There was no sign of him.

We'd booked two buses. Finally just one battered old thing arrived, coughing to a stop after crawling up the dirt road, so ninety of us squashed in for the twenty-kilometre ride into town. We could wait no longer for Fermín, so our student teacher Evita took the uniform to go and fetch him and come by taxi. Not knowing exactly where he lived, we watched the girl set off alone under the already-blistering sun. I wondered how she'd ever find him, let alone flag down safe transport all the way out here.

The decrepit bus picked up its pace coasting downhill into town. Packed like sardines in a tin on a roller coaster, we hurtled through the streets while teachers yelled directions to the driver and the children kept up a valiant chorus of song. Forty-five minutes later we arrived and fell out, gasping, still more or less presentable. Around us, anxious parents from all levels of Arequipeñan society put finishing touches to their young marchers' outfits, before they lined up to await their turn to parade before the dignitaries. Brass instruments glinted in the sun, surrounded by school uniforms of grey, maroon, green, and blue; while Colegio Elohim's staff stood out in snappy red sombreros over black suits and skirts.

Just moments before they began their march-past, Fermín arrived in his new clothes, shoes gleaming, appearing dazed as Evita ushered him to his place and smoothed his hair. They started to move, and I ran along beside, filming as they marched past the official stands to a crackly commentary about these children in extreme poverty from a small independent school way out in the squatter settlements of Arequipa.

When the parade ended two hours later, we shepherded eighty hot, hungry, thirsty children to the firmly-padlocked gate of a shady park with flowerbeds, trees and play equipment. We peered through the metal grid at a municipal caretaker who finally heaved herself out of a canvas seat and ambled over. Rosa pleaded with her to bend the rules that leave every park locked day and night because of persistent vandalism.

As I watched, I felt a surge of sympathy for the citizens of Arequipa, young and old, locked out of parks like naughty children, and remembered other social indignities: public toilets without seats, no soap in the holders, rolls of paper hanging outside the cubicle, long queues in the cold to enter the theatre … and the ultimate insult, the sign in the ladies' at the club: 'It is forbidden to pee while showering.' How did they think they were going to police that?

The caretaker finally relented and opened up to our young marchers who collapsed sprawling on the grass out of the sun. Carolina and the kitchen mothers arrived in a yellow taxi, heaved out huge pots, and set them upon a concrete table. They began ladling steaming lentils and vegetables to famished children, teachers and parents who'd come along to help.

During lunch, Evita told me she'd arrived at Fermín's shack to find his mamá Valentina rushing off to sell on the streets, ordering her oldest son to stay home and mind the younger children. Once she'd gone, Evita had begged Fermín to come with her, promising to return with him and explain to his mother, lessening the risk of a thrashing. Fermín had agonised, but despite his terror, chosen his teacher, and they'd left the two younger siblings carefully locked inside. I cringed at the thought of it … but then, some months earlier, Valentina had gone to Cusco for a week with the baby and left Fermín to mind Alfredo in a one-roomed shack with no water, no sanitation, a kerosene stove, and no food. At age nine, Fermín had become a dab hand at preparing soup out of animal intestines.

★

The next day, Valentina came to the school to see Rosa. I sat in on the interview and watched the young woman shuffle in with an infant tied upon her back in a stained blanket which smelt strongly of sour milk. She didn't react to the news that we had won second place in the competition, a result which Fermín and his team had achieved against all odds. Indeed, she didn't appear to be listening at all. Finally, Rosa mentioned that the neighbours had been gossiping about the shouting and screams they'd heard coming from the shack, and speculating about her sons' treatment at the hands of their stepfather; who, we'd found out, regularly took them out of school to work for him.

'If you do not treat Fermín and Alfredo kindly,' said Rosa, slowly and deliberately, 'someone will report you, and the authorities will come and take them away. Do you understand?'

Valentina stared at her. Yes, she did understand; it dawned in her eyes, closely followed by cold, dark fear. She blurted out a denial, an excuse, and fell silent. After she'd left, I asked Rosa, 'Do you think she grasped a single word you said?'

'Without a doubt, one thing sank in,' she replied. 'The threat of losing her children.'

Later, bumping down the dirt track in the combi, I wrestled with the abandonment and abuse of two little boys by their mother and stepfather; and the fact that the adults' greatest fear was the removal the offspring they so mistreated. Of course, I reminded myself, I had to make allowances for the cruel culture of poverty … but for Fermín, Alfredo and their younger sister, the refuge offered by our school may be the only way out of the cycle. To use the teacher Isabella's words, the only escape from eventually turning into their parents.

CHAPTER 30

The edges of the poster on the outside wall of the school fluttered in the desert breeze. 'Campaña Médica' it announced in bright red capital letters. Shortly after our triumph in the marching competition, a local Rotary club had organised a medical campaign to be held at Colegio Elohim.

On the designated Sunday morning a large group of volunteers – doctors, an ophthalmologist, dentists, psychologists, cosmetology and hairdressing students – headed out in a convoy of buses to offer free services to the community of Héroes del Cenepa. Having always travelled on the milk-run combi, I panicked when I realised that the leading driver thought I knew the way. Fortunately, a few recognisable landmarks and some lucky guesses eventually led us up through the dusty maze and onto the final kilometres of familiar dirt road. Passing throngs of people heading on foot to the school, I waved from the bus window and called out, 'See you very soon at the campaign!' They were all coming. Our intensive publicity efforts had paid off. We came to a triumphant halt outside the school ... and the truth dawned.

We had agreed the date weeks in advance, consulting with the municipal authorities and the local dirigente, the boss of the squatter area, before putting up the posters and handing out flyers. We all went home at 2 pm on Friday, with everything organised for the event on the Sunday. At 5 pm, without our knowledge, the local boss had announced a compulsory meeting for the residents on the basketball court opposite the school – to be held at exactly the same time as the proposed medical campaign. This was where the crowds had been heading, so we arrived to find almost all our potential customers locked into an obligatory reunion they didn't dare leave. El dirigente had decided to show us who was boss. Never mind that we were helping his community; he didn't see it that way. Perhaps he had expected us to pay for his co-operation ... it was not uncommon for these individuals to muster crowds of tens of thousands to march in protest for whichever side of a cause – whether mining, property, national politics, or a local scandal – was prepared to pay the most.

Undeterred, we started setting up stands and equipment in the classrooms. I had but one objective – to secure an ophthalmology appointment for Fermín. After an hour he had not appeared, so I grabbed two teachers, explaining my mission, and before losing my courage, charged with them up into the hills. A group of excited children bounded alongside us to show the way.

We arrived at his shack and called him, staying outside the gate in case a mongrel went for us. The child emerged from the dark interior, grubby, ragged, bare foot. 'Come with us,' I called cheerfully, 'there's a doctor who can check your eyes.'

He mumbled that he couldn't because, 'Mi mamá has gone out and said I had to mind Alfredo and the baby while she's asleep inside.'

'Let's all go together,' I suggested, getting desperate, but this idea terrified him even more, knowing the beating he'd get if his mother returned to the shack to find it empty.

At this point, entirely by chance, Valentina did in fact arrive. I explained about the campaña, and she spluttered out some clearly negative references to cooking, working and Fermín minding the children. Thanks to my limited supply of curses in castellano, I remained reasonably polite. 'Valentina, you have a responsibility to care for your children. Fermín and Alfredo must come with us right now to see the eye doctor.'

She turned her blank gaze on me, muttered something about lunch, and went inside, summoning Fermín to follow her. The poor little boy stood still in confusion. At this point, I stormed into the gloomy shack and yelled at her in the best Peruvian slang I could muster, 'If you had any sense, you'd be down there at the head of the queue with all three of your children, giving thanks that some caring people want to help you!'

Whatever I did actually say, or perhaps the tone of my voice, had the desired effect. We finally set off with Fermín and Alfredo skipping beside us in laceless sand-shoes down the rubbish-strewn path toward the school. By the time we arrived at 1 pm, the dirigente, having run out of agenda items for his captive audience, had ended his meeting and medical business had picked up. Long queues had formed outside each of the specialists' doors, just as the allotted campaign time neared its end, and exhausted volunteers began looking forward to heading home for what remained of their Sunday. I secured the last two appointments with the ophthalmologist for Fermín and Alfredo.

The two brothers sat wonderstruck as the doctor tried different lenses and asked them to read the chart, finally prescribing strong spectacles for both and exercises to improve Fermín's squint. A few weeks later, I collected the glasses from the clinic in town, giving strict instructions that they remain at school, only to be worn during class. I doubted anyone would oversee the eye exercises; but for the moment, at least, I congratulated myself on a small triumph in the battle for Fermín and his brother.

★

One morning several weeks later, I found Rosa hard at work poring over the computer screen in her office with Isabella who, as well as teacher of Grade 2, was the staff expert in necessary-IT-for-urgent-documents-for-the-Ministerio-de-Educación. She was trying to detect and rectify faults in the database for something doubtless due days earlier, and she'd left her boisterous class of thirty-two in the hands of her assistant. I intuited that this was definitely not the moment for yet another of Miss Susi's lectures about duty of care, now a legal requirement in Peru. Instead, I headed for the classroom.

Most of the children were noisily at work on a task Isabella had left them, the assistant moving around to help ... but some wandered, unwilling, or unable, to write captions for the picture story. I sat down with one boy and, as he dictated, I wrote, in the looped cursive style, with its confusing 'r', 'n' and 'm'. This I'd had to re-learn since coming to Peru, Australian schools having changed to modified cursive when I'd been in Grade 3. I asked the seven year olds round the table for help with some of my shaky spelling, and one little boy eyed me curiously. 'Mees Soosi, who taught you to speak castellano?'

'I learned it by myself,' I replied, 'listening to you all and copying what you say; trying to understand, reading lots and studying my vocabulary and grammar book.'

I found my way to Alfredo, in stained T-shirt, worn track pants, shoes without laces and no socks. He was trying to tear the page out of his book in quiet frustration. 'Don't worry, it's all right,' I reassured him and found some tape to repair the damage. 'Where are your glasses?'

He pointed, and I went over to where, sure enough, they sat safely on the shelf, where they'd probably been since the last time I had visited the classroom. He put them on, assuring me with vigorous nods that, yes, he could see better. Then I knelt on the floor beside him and we began his story. 'What were the boys doing?' I asked.

'Fishing in the river,' he replied. I listened as he expressed himself in words I could understand, and transcribe for him. He still had a long way to go before he could write alone or read his work back to me, but he'd made much progress over twelve months. He sketched two stick figures in a boat with rods.

'What should we put in the water?' I asked.

'Truchas,' he said. So we both began drawing trout.

Mine took on gargantuan proportions, dwarfing the humans. 'Help! They're colossal!' I exclaimed. 'Those fishermen had better watch out, hadn't they?'

He slid me a shy sideways glance and his face creased into a broad grin.

★

During that week, the Primary grades went on a town excursion to the library, once again, and the Plaza de Armas, where I stood with Fermín before the three-tiered fountain, watching the pigeons diving and splashing.

'How would it feel to be one of them?' I asked, and we talked about their privileged existence. The public fed them. Pigeons, not people, were allowed to strut on the fenced-off grass in the shade, and hop into the cool water. If they didn't want to stay, they could simply take off. 'Just think, Fermín, you'd never feel hungry, you could have a swim, or even fly away, whenever you wanted. Bueno, no?' He smiled and it occurred to me that the feathered creatures enjoyed a far better life than this neglected little boy.

I visited Fermín in Grade 3 a few days later and he showed me two drawings from the town excursion: the library garden and the fountain. I wrote the titles, which he copied accurately. His drawings showed talent, especially considering they'd been done by a child with severe sight problems and a squint. His glasses had not been in the classroom for months: it seemed he had accidentally taken them home one day and his mother had kept them, forbidding him to take them back to school because he'd break them. On that same day, I visited Alfredo again, only to learn that his spectacles, too, had left the premises and found their way into Valentina's hands. In her logic of extreme poverty, precious things had to be preserved, not used.

I prepared a translation of parts of the International Rights of the Child for every parent to read or have read to them, and sign or mark with a thumbprint when enrolling their children. When the brothers' stepfather arrived and Rosa asked about their regular absences from school, he replied, 'Aye, Señorita, I take them with me, to work and learn how to earn a living.' The boys were hauling desert sand, unpaid, on building sites.

One of the teachings of the Tao suggests that sometimes it's best to do nothing and things will change by themselves. Over time they did, and I learned a lesson about being judgmental. Once again we visited Fermín's shack to be greeted by Valentina with a relatively clean toddler scampering around her feet and a new baby, her fifth, upon her back. Leading us through an orderly yard past hanging washing, she showed off her vegetable garden, where corn, beans, alfalfa, spinach, potatoes and pumpkin thrived in the desert sand. Opposite, she pointed out Fermín and Alfredo's own room away from the rest of the family.

By then, her third child attended kindergarten

at Colegio Elohim, Rosa having reassured her that it didn't matter if she couldn't pay the enrolment fee straight away; beginning her daughter's education was more important. Valentina beamed as I mentioned Fermín's smart appearance at school in his pressed white shirt, clean pants and knotted tie, and praised his skills since he'd started helping in his uncle's fledgling bakery nearby.

I realised that in those tense early days of our relationship, she'd probably understood as little of me as I had of her … especially given my level of castellano. The time had come to revise my initial impressions of Valentina.

CHAPTER 31

The verse echoed out over the listening congregation. 'The Father who dwells in me does his works. Believe me … but if you do not, then believe me because of the works themselves.'

August 15th had arrived, marking the town's 474th anniversary of Spanish settlement and with Antonio not keen to face the crowds, I'd set off alone to witness for myself the famous parade, el Corso de la Amistad. Walking along Santa Catalina, I'd noticed open doors adjoining the monastery and slipped into the chapel, cool and laden with incense, to find a mass in progress. Hearing the nuns' pure voices singing from behind a plaited screen, I'd remembered my first months in Arequipa, when, staying nearby in the hostel, I'd often come to hear the matins of the closed order. The hymn over, one of the sisters had just finished the reading from a pulpit. Now, clearly visible through the lattice just a metre away from me, she closed the bible and her grey eyes met mine with a smile.

The service over, I stepped out into the sun, joining a moving crowd as I passed by stalls and ambulant sellers of collapsible stools, sunhats and parasols. I finally reached the parade and found myself caught up in it, the sides of the road so tightly jammed with spectators that I couldn't stop and squeeze in among them. Even slowing down brought cries of 'Avance!' urging me to move along as I obstructed those who'd been there since dawn. Finally spotting a chink on the kerb, I darted over and wiggled my behind into it, sinking onto soggy tickertape and grime as people beside shifted to accommodate me. I had found my place, where I'd remain without moving for the next three hours.

Boys and girls danced in brightly-coloured satin to brass band music belting out from loud speakers in a tico taxi covered with streamers. Blouses and skirts swirled past, long black plaits, flying capes, tailored pants, leather boots and wide straw hats. Laughing teenagers skipped with effortless steps, as much a part of their lives as the Coke they took time out to swig and the mobile phones which appeared from hidden pockets for quick calls. Las Tunas followed – not marine life, but male groups from universities all over South America, dressed like minstrels in black doublets and stockings, their capes sporting coloured ribbons from each place they'd visited. They crooned traditional songs, silly ditties and heartbreaking ballads, strumming on guitars, violins and mandolins, pan flutes and drums.

Next came the Ccapo, the bush of Chachani which over centuries has always been brought down from the foothills in August on donkeys. The patient creatures in flowered bridles plodded past, bearing cane baskets of dried branches and leaves used for lighting fires. A semi-trailer rumbled behind, decked out like a traditional country market with paper and plywood trees and vegetable stalls, where damsels served plastic cups of corn chicha beer from enormous kegs. Ducks poked around at their feet, while two fighting cocks, chained far apart, strained to attack each other. Several Paso horses trotted nimbly after the vehicle, with riders in woven ponchos, and finally, two enormous bulls.

Glamorous girls in 'Miss Arequipa' sashes hurled handfuls of sweets into the crowd. Peruvians from the jungle jumped and gyrated in outfits of feathers and not much else. Others, in jeans and sunglasses with caps on backwards, boogied to the latest homeboy hits in blaring Peruvian reggaetón. Behind them frolicked clowns of all sizes, a rainbow of painted faces and pointed hats with outlandish masks, flinging powder bombs, bubbles and confetti.

All the while, the informal parade of street-sellers passed by, paying scant attention to the entertainment. Offering snacks to the spectators, or blowing bubbles from coloured pipes to entertain restless children, they struggled to sell on the goods they had bought at the market, to make some profit on an investment they could scarcely afford.

A red-faced, sweating boy in a baseball cap clutched the handles of a large metal baking dish, staggering under its weight, as he trailed along in the hot sun behind his mother. She, too, hauled a tray; like her son's, groaning with pastel de papa, oven-browned potato bake. The man behind me yelled out, 'How much?'

'Dos soles cincuenta la porción,' replied the woman.

Clearly considering two soles fifty excessive for a generous helping, he shouted, 'Un sol!', but she shook her head and he waved her away with a jerk of his hand.

I thought of Flora Linda in Grade 6. Sweet-natured, a lovely flower as her name implied, abandoned by her mother years ago, she lived with her father, an ice-cream salesman. The previous week at school, as we stood intertwined in a bear hug, I'd asked her if she'd be going to the parade.

'Yes,' she'd replied, 'with my papá.' Not, I knew, for a fun day out, but rather to help him offering paddlepops at fifty centimos each. At least they wouldn't weigh as much as the trays of potato bake. Like Flora Linda, most of our students would be out selling with their parents at the parade when potential customers thronged the streets; indeed, Rosa had suspended the following day's classes, knowing they'd be too exhausted to come to school.

At 3 pm I walked home along streets for once devoid of traffic to watch the final hours of the procession on TV in the comfort of my home.

★

'Rosa! Those buildings are ready to topple!' I gasped.

'Please God not on top of any of the children!' she cried.

'And we can't do a thing about them until we get the chance to buy back the land they're built on!'

A week after the procession, we stared out over exactly half the total area of the school, untouchable, embargoed by the furious accountant so many years earlier for his fees unpaid when the elderly gringo absconded with lover and funds. From the balcony of the new three-storey classroom building on one side, we could see four crumbling structures sitting in the dust on the other. We needed to regain ownership of the land to build a second, adequate wing, but this could only happen when the public registry ordered an auction ... and for six long years, the case had languished, buried deep in dark corridors, with no prospect of emerging any time soon. It could take up to twenty years, our lawyer Doctor Nuñez had warned.

'Aye,' moaned Rosa. 'I have heard that the old señor

gringo is still alive and he and his wife own seven houses in Arequipa. All bought with our donation money which they stole. If only he had used some of it to pay his actuary's bill, at least the whole school would still belong to us, instead of half.'

I shook my head and sighed. The increase in support since donations had become tax-deductible had meant that enough money for further construction sat in the bank account, ready to go. 'We can only wait,' I said. 'All that time ago, Colegio Elohim used a donation to legally buy the land … but now, it no longer belongs to us. In fact, it doesn't belong to anyone.'

In November, I flew back to Sydney to catch Rachel before she headed off to Europe for her second season working in the ski fields. For twelve days, I had all four children within a ten-kilometre radius, spending time with them separately and together, culminating in a champagne picnic in the Botanic Gardens … a highlight in my memory of our harbour city at its very best, and the joy of being reunited with my family after so long apart.

Conversation flowed easily and without reference to difficult recent times until Rachel, at lunch alone with me one day, finally came out with the words she'd kept silent for five years. 'Mum, you left!'

I gave a weak reply, something along the lines of, 'I didn't feel I had any choice' ... of course not strictly true; I left because I wanted to. I added that over the years I'd apologised as best I could: about leaving, about selling the house, about everything; and couldn't spend the rest of my days feeling guilty ... words from my head which my heart wasn't yet altogether convinced about. At that moment, she told me years later, she felt everything come out into the open, and she realised she could move on. I hoped I had been unconditionally forgiven.

Too soon, I drove her to the airport and watched her, tall, slim and athletic, heave the snowboard into the oversized luggage cage and check herself in. I hugged her at the familiar passengers-only departure gate, unsure when we'd cross paths again. 'See you, Mumsie,' she smiled. Before I could weep, with a toss of blonde hair she was gone, off on her own adventure.

CHAPTER 32

Back in Arequipa the following January, I relaxed into my pillows and opened up a book on Spanish grammar I'd bought in Sydney. The leaky roof finally fixed, I had injured my back and then caught the flu, ending up in bed for almost three weeks. This gave me the opportunity to apply myself to some study. I knew that my ignorance of how to issue commands meant that I'd been confusing my pupils at Colegio Elohim for years. For example, 'you are sitting down' does not mean 'sit down!' Just as in English, this is a command, and needs to be expressed as such. So, for example, if Alex in Grade 6 was standing up, and I said to him 'te sientas', I was in fact telling him 'you are sitting down', rather than commanding, 'sit down!'. He of course would stare at me in bafflement: 'I'm not sitting down, I'm standing up,' … and he'd be right. No wonder he never sat down.

With the help of the book, I began to weave through

the labyrinth of commands and, once I returned to school, every time I had to 'order' a child to do something, I'd stop, pause, think, then come triumphantly out with it, 'Open your book! Fetch me your pen! Stand up and go outside!' ... by which time the moment had been lost and everyone had moved on ... but, ever so slowly, it all began to stick.

I continued reading, meditating and resting up for an 800 kilometre pilgrimage. With an Australian friend, I planned to follow the footsteps of the apostle Santiago and complete the Camino across the north of Spain. I set the walk up as a fundraising page on the internet in aid of Colegio Elohim; causing some confusion among my Arequipeñan friends. Unfamiliar with the concept of sponsoring physical efforts for a cause, they couldn't understand what my walking the Camino had to do with a school in the town's slums. In fact, most thought I wanted them to donate money so I could have a holiday in Spain. Eventually, with much careful explanation that I would be paying my own way and any money raised would go to Colegio Elohim, I managed to collect $400 in cash locally; leaving the web donation page to my international contacts.

We completed the installation of our twenty brand-new computers in the laboratory, created by closing in a patio; I took photos and sent out a supporters' bulletin featuring children clicking mouses, interacting with mathematics, spelling, colours, and health education on the screens. Around this time, Rosa asked me to show teachers the methodologies she had observed in my English classes, which corresponded to the student-centred learning now officially adopted by the Ministerio de Educación. So after checking the Spanish translations for 'pair work' and 'teacher talk' I launched into my first training session in castellano. This time, encouraged by the backing of the Peruvian state education authority, I delved deep into the outcomes-based pupil assessment system I had used for over a decade in Australia, aided by innovative resources available online at the Ministry website. I offered to do more, excited by the prospect of drawing on my classroom experience to further share my knowledge of multiple intelligences, hands-on learning, and classroom management. The new professional strand I'd begun in Nepal in English and continued in Rwanda in French, would now culminate in Peru in Spanish.

Out of the blue, at the end of March, came the sort of fluke occurrence which, if this story were not true, would have readers muttering about stretching credibility to suit plot needs. Rosa heard something from the cousin of the mother of a friend who worked shuffling papers in the bowels of the public registry, the Poder Judicial ... the case of the embargoed land had started moving. We hurried to our lawyer and sure enough, something, at last, seemed to be happening. Over the next few weeks, the proceedings advanced to the final stage, at which the furious accountant simply had to formally instruct the Judiciary to proceed with the auction. We dared to hope that things may soon be coming to a head.

The date of my departure on the pilgrimage came ever closer. We celebrated an Easter Pageant and Mother's Day, and completed all preparations for Rosa, as legal representative, to participate in the auction, which would surely take place during my absence. On May 12th, I pulled on my walking books and backpack, and headed out of the door, bound for northern Spain.

Two months later, back in Arequipa, I posted a message with photos of a path, 875 kilometres and thirty-seven days long, winding its way through mountain forests covered in snow and rolling hills basking in sunshine, past tiny stone villages, elegant cities and magnificent cathedrals. Consuming considerable quantities of vino tinto y blanco along the way, we'd reached Santiago Cathedral, to join in the culminating mass: inhaling the smoky fragrance of the enormous silver incense diffuser as it swung back and forth over our heads on ropes hauled by five priests. At the end of the service, watching the church doors heave open and daylight flood into the gloom, I sobbed with the overwhelming realisation that I stood on the threshold of the rest of my life.

As a wonderful surprise, Rachel had joined us for the last ninety kilometres beyond Santiago to Finisterra. On the penultimate night, she sat on her top bunk in her skins, long hair falling forward as she chatted in German to the portly middle-aged male cyclist who'd pedalled from Hamburg. I threw in the odd bit of pidgin Deutsch laced with Spanish, while my friend beneath me added her bit in English. It was the perfect pilgrimage tableau.

Loyal support from international contacts on the web sponsorship page, plus the cash contribution from my friends in Arequipa, raised over $11,000 for the children of Colegio Elohim.

Upon returning to Arequipa, I'd expected news about the successful re-purchase of the embargoed land at auction; but it had all ground to a halt. Everything we'd planned to move the school forward remained on hold until we regained ownership of that land. If we didn't get it back, and soon, we could go no further.

Antonio and I loved the idea of travelling together and still planned local trips, ever hopeful we could overcome the problems we now had spending more than a day in each other's company. During July, his annual holiday month, we set out for a week in the jungle town of Iquitos, in northeastern Peru, accessible only by plane from Lima or a week-long boat trip. We found it hot, humid, dirty and mosquito-ridden; the only pleasant part being sections of its riverside boulevard. Here, occasional tiled palatial residences from the era of the rubber boom still stood alongside cafés with views across muddy, quiet waters; enjoyed by gringos left over from the hippy era.

We escaped to a jungle lodge where we sprawled in hammocks on a netted verandah, surrounded by the buzz and click of unseen hordes of insects. In gumboots and protective clothing we splashed through the steamy rainforest to find ancient, soaring trees. Among them, the remains of plantations, whose bark when cut still oozed the latex which, decades earlier, had made fortunes for the Peruvian barons … and caused unspeakable suffering to the local indigenous people contracted as slave labour. We cruised the mighty Amazon, pink freshwater porpoises diving alongside, and visited a self-sufficient village. Here, excited children told us the history of Peru they'd been learning in their hut school; before racing with us to the river for a swim. At night, lying cosy and dry in bed, we listened to thunderous tropical downpours pelting the thatch above our heads.

★

No matter how promising it all appeared on the outside, everything changed on the third evening when I declined a pisco sour after dinner. Antonio's mood darkened, and didn't improve. I gave into exhausted despair and as soon as we returned to Iquitos, I rebooked my flight from Lima back to Arequipa two days earlier. When I finally plucked up the courage to tell him, he remained silent for several seconds, then uttered slowly and deliberately, 'You're ending our relationship.'

It's hard to stay near someone when you're fighting, but travelling far from home, we had to. The next afternoon, we arrived at Iquitos Airport for the return flight to Lima, to find the plane delayed. As we waited, I watched Antonio engrossed in his book, clearly a distressing tale. Every so often he put it down, removed his glasses, took out his handkerchief and dabbed his eyes. He'd get up and take a walk around the terminal, returning to sink back into his seat and sigh, 'Ayayay,' before picking up the tragedy once more. I smiled … inappropriately, given the current rupture could be our last.

We arrived in Lima at 9.30 pm, and took a taxi to his sister's flat. Antonio, still distant and angry, hardly glanced at me. When we finally went to our room, I sat on the bed and waited.

Eventually, he said softly, 'Is this all my fault?'

'We're both to blame.'

'But we're two intelligent adults, aren't we? Why can't we work this out?'

The pisco sour incident had provoked suspicion and confrontation, but I couldn't face stirring it all up again, so chose instead to focus on our cultural differences. 'It's because we're adults that we can't work it out. We've both raised families with other partners over decades in countries half a world apart, and now we're old and set in our different ways. We can't change because we don't want to.'

He gazed at me sorrowfully. 'I'm selfish, jealous and petulant.'

I reached for his hand and squeezed it. 'No more than I am. We're friends, not enemies. I don't want to hurt you, and you don't want to hurt me.'

He leaned over to kiss me. As I felt his warm lips, I once again gave in to hope.

The following morning the taxi didn't turn up and we realised we'd have to call one from the kerb – possibly even more risky in Lima than in Arequipa.

'Why can't a policeman take me? Where are they when you need them?' I grumbled, half-serious. We eventually flagged one down, and Antonio made a show of copying down the number plate, waving and calling, 'Ring me when you get to the airport.'

As usual, I sat in the front, telling the young driver of my nervousness and my kidnap. 'Ah, no!' he said, and out of the glovebox pulled his policeman's badge. He earned extra cash driving in his spare time. I stifled a burst of laughter, and we spent the rest of the trip chatting about Colegio Elohim and the kids he counselled as part of his job until we reached the airport.

I flew back to Arequipa and over the following days thought much about my years with Antonio; of the romance and promise of our earliest outings and weekends around Arequipa, and of the joyful adventure of the Santa Cruz trek. I forced myself to remember our time in Francisco Mostajo and the damage wreaked as our deepest secrets and prejudices had emerged. Although since then we'd spent several holidays together, I finally admitted to myself that every one had been tainted by a clash and its consequences. By now, although I had never found any proof, there was little doubt in my mind that alcohol was the secret ingredient that exacerbated the irritability, the anger and the moods; and I wasn't at all proud of the way I reacted to them. The events at Iquitos had simply been yet another repetition of a sad, inevitable pattern.

CHAPTER 33

Some months later, twenty Rotarians from the US visited Colegio Elohim with a specific job in mind – to cover two hundred brand-new Spanish primary reading books they had funded, some sent from the States and others bought locally. This assistance had begun when my meditation companion Patricia had introduced me to her childhood friend and tennis partner, a retired surgeon who'd married and left Peru to live in Chicago forty-nine years earlier. He had returned to Arequipa more than seventy-five times since, bringing funds, equipment and medical experts to build up the burns unit of the Hospital General to a world-class standard. By the time I met the eminent doctor he was in his mid-seventies. Full of enthusiasm, he travelled out to Colegio Elohim, astonishing and delighting the kitchen mothers with lusty renditions of songs in their indigenous Quechua. He'd learned the language in Cusco as a child, where his father, also a medical practitioner, had spent many years serving disadvantaged local communities. At the end of the school visit, he pledged support for our cause, and together with his wife, brought on board three Rotary clubs in the US, eager to engage in projects over the years to come, donations to be channelled through the local club in Arequipa.

The week after the departure of the cheerful, hardworking group of volunteers, I stepped inside the gate of Colegio Elohim to find a crowd of four year olds bouncing around in the courtyard, their room firmly locked. Seeing the class aide rushing to the girls' toilet with a bucket, I asked the teacher what had happened.

'Tomasito threw the keys away,' she replied with an embarrassed smile. 'Yesterday, he stole the music teacher Anna's change and left her with no fare for the combi home.'

Tomasito had arrived at Colegio Elohim five years earlier, aged four, with severe learning and behavioural difficulties. His single mother worked as a cleaner to support her children, so he spent long afternoons after school in their shack with just his two older sisters. His father had abandoned them, leaving the lonely little boy with a fixation on adult males; indeed, on one town excursion as our students crowded onto a pavement, a man wading through them suddenly stopped, startled, as Tomasito's arms locked tight around him in a bear hug.

While in kindergarten, his academic level was manageable, but not his behaviour. He'd hit out at his class mates, stealing their food and gobbling it down, even pulling used chewing gum out of the bin to stuff it into his mouth. He graduated into Grade 1, repeated, and finished far behind his peers, still unable to read or write a word. His nose was always running, face and hands grimy, feet dusty and clad in the traditional rubber sandals of the poorest rural folk. He spent time with Rosa in her office, where she gave him simple games and tasks to try and improve his letters and numbers. Meanwhile, he grew taller and stronger, and as time went on, he moved to a favourite spot on the floor in the back of Yulissa's Grade 6 class, where he built Lego – until he got bored and wandered off. Things started disappearing – colourful toys and equipment from the infants' rooms, books from primary shelves – and we'd find them in all sorts of odd places, as Tomasito went about 'tidying up'. When he took to re-organising keys, and money from purses, the trouble began in earnest.

On that particular morning, I found the teacher's aide scooping water out of the huge drum in the girls' toilet. At its bottom, glinting through the ripples, sat the bunch of classroom master keys. Just then, the culprit came bustling in with another smaller bucket and began to help with the bailing.

I took the pail out of his hands and searched his face. 'Tomasito,' I said, slowly and clearly, 'do you know what you have done? This special water from the tanker truck has been wasted, and all the children and their teacher can't go into class – because of what you did. And do you know what happened to Miss Anna yesterday after you took her money? She had no fare for the combi and she had to walk home down the hill in the dust.' I doubted whether in fact she had, but Tomasito's face dropped. When we'd finally retrieved the keys, I made him scoop all the water back. He then sat in the cubby house to have a think about what he'd done.

At the end of the morning, he came loping up to me as I walked down the dusty track to catch the bus. 'Miss Anna had no money for the combi,' he said.

'No, she didn't,' I replied, and turning on my way I added, 'Chau, Tomasito.'

The following week, Rosa and I heard a turning in the lock on her office door. We jumped up and found ourselves imprisoned. 'Tomasito!' we both yelled, and heard it unlock with a click. We pushed the door open to catch a glimpse of him charging down the corridor; and Rosa stopped leaving keys in doors. A few days later I saw him whack a tot of five over the head with a plastic bottle – so hard she staggered before bursting into tears – and then give her a huge hug after I yelled at him.

Our young psychologist administered diagnostic tests which Rosa presented to the Ministerio de Educación, requesting support in transferring Tomasito to a special school, but she was instructed to integrate him. Eventually, pressure from parents forced her to speak to his mother. We knew that the abandoned single woman would unlikely have the means to support her son in a special-needs institution, even if a place could be found. A vision of Tomasito haunted me – obedient, simple and extremely strong, a loyal asset to any gang.

Tomasito did not return for the next academic year, spending his days alone inside his hovel while his mother went out to work. One day I spotted him, crouched near the school gates like an old, mad tramp; spinning back toward the pitiful physical and mental destitution of his earliest days at Colegio Elohim. I waved but he ran away, and there was nothing I could do about it.

Soon after, a call came from the lawyer announcing a date for our auction: November 27th. In a flurry we finalised the plans with our architect for construction to begin as soon as we had the land. The new building would contain a level of classrooms offering a special secondary technical option for our most abandoned ex-students, past and future. Paulo; Veronica, Lucía and their younger siblings; Fermín, Alfredo and their sisters, to name but a few. Workrooms for vocational training in electricity, hairdressing, cosmetology, cooking and sewing for a start, not only for our primary graduates, but also for parents, with child-care provided. A stationery and grocery store to begin earning income for the school, and a new kitchen.

A week later, with all the necessary documentation finalised for the approaching land sale, Rosa, Yulissa and I met with Doctor Nuñez. Once we had run through the procedure for the day, we chatted about why the case had come to light and eventually reached this crucial stage; given that it could have remained buried for decades. Rosa and Yulissa had no doubt whatsoever who'd had a hand in it.

'Of course, it is la mano de Dios, because He listens to children, and the whole school has been praying for months.'

Doctor Nuñez, part of the conservative Catholic establishment of Arequipa, spoke of his belief that in the end divine justice will prevail.

'Estimado Doctor Nuñez,' I said. 'The elderly gringo and his wife now own seven properties which they bought with our donations, and we've been forced into this expensive, stressful process to re-purchase the land we already owned. Where's the divine justice in that?'

'Señora Soosan, I do not believe that Heaven and Hell await us at the end; we live them, here, and now.' He paused. 'I'd heard nothing of the elderly señor for years, but just the other day I saw him in the street, in a wheelchair, being pushed by his wife. He appeared senile and dazed, and must be one hundred years old, while his wife would be just forty. No number of houses could compensate for the fact that the old man didn't die when he was supposed to, leaving her free, extremely wealthy, and still young … he lives on, in a nightmare of his own, and she's there with him, every hour, every day. They don't need to go to Hell, they're in it already.'

I found this interpretation rather appealing, and a smug thought popped into my head. If we got the land on November 27th and allowed two weeks for legal transfer of ownership, we could lay the first stone of the new construction on December 16th, my sixtieth birthday. *How poetic.*

The day after that memorable meeting, the judges and administrative staff of the Poder Judicial went on strike, nationally and indefinitely, for better work conditions.

★

The date set for our auction came and went. While meditating the following morning, I found myself in a glade facing a small buddha who placed a tiny carved wooden box into my hand. I opened it to find a plain, pure white impatiens flower. I bent to smell it, but of course it had no scent. As I pondered what my subconscious was communicating to me, I made a connection with my garden. Soon after moving in to the cottage two years before, I had stopped paying monthly rent and instead negotiated an *anti-cresis* with my landlady; basically, making her an interest-free loan, in exchange for use of the little house gratis for the period. I had hoped to be able to extend it, but had recently received notice to leave, as she intended to refurbish it. I'd decided to make the most of every minute left, writing, editing, and taking time to contemplate the jacaranda, the pine trees sighing in the afternoon breeze, and sun and shade playing on the green grass.

But why an impatiens, without a smell? For me, a flower is not complete without a scent. Finally I understood the message. Things would eventually turn out … but not necessarily as I wanted or expected.

The following week, I revisited the verse I'd heard on my way to Arequipa's anniversary procession, read by the young nun in the monastery chapel. 'The Father who dwells in me does his works. Believe me … but if you do not, then believe me because of the works themselves.' I thought of Rosa and Yulissa and their unshakeable Christian faith; of Dr Nuñez and his ideas about justice; of my eclectic religious persuasions; and of the 'works' which brought us all together – the children of Colegio Elohim.

CHAPTER 34

I stood before the portable two-ring stove and attached gas bottle, wondering what to do with it and the laundry basins, kitchen utensils, and few pieces of furniture I owned. Just ten days remained until I was to leave the garden cottage. I'd already wrapped the Peruvian clay pottery securely in metres of paper and tape, ready for the suitcase and the long journey to the Sydney storage next time I visited.

'I may need these if I end up in unfurnished accommodation next year,' I was musing when a knock came on the door. I opened it and found my landlady, who invited me to sit with her on the seat outside in the morning sunshine.

'Soosi,' she began, 'I've been in such chaos, aye Dios mío, and now my plans have changed. You never know what life will bring, do you?' She smiled. 'I've decided to postpone the restoration of your cottage. Would you prefer to stay?'

For several seconds, I gaped at her, the white impatiens flower slipping into my mind. I blinked and nodded vigorously, 'Yes! That would suit me perfectly.' The urge to hoot with laughter and turn cartwheels all over the lawn nearly got the better of me.

The following week, Antonio and I made the four-hour bus journey through snow-tipped volcanic ranges to Colca Canyon for a Christmas treat at a luxury hotel. We strolled hand in hand in the lush grounds, wandering through terraced green hills, and lazing in steaming pools fed by boiling springs out of bare rock. We walked to the nearby settlement of Yanque on Christmas Day, to watch the villagers dancing the Wititi. Both men and women swirled through the streets in long colourful skirts and embroidered hats, the female costumes having been used long ago to smuggle local lads out under the noses of the invading Spanish. Lines of minstrels with pipes, trumpets and drums followed, their exuberant music ringing out all over the valley. Earthenware barrels of chicha beer sat ready for the thirsty performers to consume over the following three days, and nights, of the festival. Only half in jest did Antonio propose, 'Soosita, I'll stay here and you collect me in three days, ya?'

I shook my head and instead we celebrated with a

champagne picnic on the terrace outside our room. I gave him a traditional miniature nativity scene set inside a tiny painted wooden box. 'Small and portable. Every Christmas it will be with you,' I'd written on the card. A fleeting shadow darkened his eyes, and with a play on the word 'esperar' which means 'wait' and also 'expect', he said, *'No olvides que te espero, y no esperes que te olvide.* Don't forget that I am waiting for you, and don't expect me to forget you.'

Our brief Christmas holiday having passed peacefully, I took the pleasant memory back to Sydney. I'd booked a cheap New Year's Eve flight from Arequipa to spend two months there. The morning before I left, I sat in bed with birdsong and jasmine incense, reading these words from an American Zoto Zen priest. 'I am learning how to feel the currents of my life … I trust that river … the more one trusts and responds, the more life shows you the way.'

In Sydney there were plenty of reminders that I didn't have to travel to developing countries to find suffering. Within my circle of friends and acquaintances, many families and individuals were facing serious illness, bereavement, emotional, psychological and physical anguish, albeit behind the closed doors of pleasant dwellings with water, sanitation and electricity. I was the lucky one to have been able to leave and set out on what was, after all, an exotic adventure.

The river meandered on, taking me with it. I finally bought the apartment I'd eventually return to, if or when the right time came. It had been waiting patiently, situated on a rise just two hundred metres away from our old family home, with glimpses of it from the balcony through trees. Staring out on the morning of the purchase, I spotted a sliver of shimmering water view beyond the pink house where over two decades of my life as wife and mother had been laid down. 'I've never even noticed that,' said the agent ... as I remembered the night, many years before, when I'd stood on a rock overhang at the end of the point and momentarily considered leaping into the salty blackness.

High on the apartment verandah above my old home, I reflected that we'd never had a view of the harbour. Now I gazed down upon my previous life, out over the turmoil which followed its demise, and on to the water with the unknown beyond. Finally, I recognised the balance and beauty of the whole picture.

The agent broke into my thoughts, announcing loudly, 'The auction is about to begin. All bidders please take your seats.'

Some weeks later, the day before handing over my new apartment to tenants and heading back to Arequipa, I drank a champagne toast with Katy, Peter and Lisa on the sheltered balcony. We snapped a photo to send to Rachel, teaching in Berlin, and I felt a circle close, as a chapter of my tale came to an end.

★

While I was in Sydney, piped water finally reached Héroes del Cenepa after five years of rumours and disappointments. I returned in March to find a sink connected outside Colegio Elohim's kitchen, with all taps, and two showers, soon to become functional in the bathrooms. The meagre supply meant the toilets still flushed by bucket, but all the same, the children washing their hands from a tap was something I hadn't thought I'd live to see.

News reached us of Tomasito. Rosa had threatened to report his mother for abandonment if she continued leaving him alone in the shack. She'd finally agreed to co-operate and, incredibly, they'd found him a special, free school in the area, close to his mamá's place of work, so she could take him and bring him home. The problem seemed to have been solved, at least for the present.

Absolutely nothing was happening at the Poder Judicial, where the employees had threatened to upgrade to a hunger strike if their demands were not soon met. Rosa, of all people, suggested that perhaps it would be better if they all starved, so a staff prepared to do some work could take their place.

★

Antonio and I travelled up into the altiplano to spend
Easter Thursday and Friday in a traditional village.
Each evening he stayed in reading at the hotel, while
I attended mass in the ancient stone church, shivering
beside the traditionally-dressed, plaited mamachas,
their shoulders warm in double-folded blankets,
legs snug in thick woollen stockings and skirts. On
Easter Thursday, the priest bathed the feet of twelve
worshippers in a re-enactment of the Last Supper, after
which youngsters in jeans and fleece jackets moved
around the pews with large cane baskets full of candles
in protectors made out of coloured tissue paper. The
congregation moved outside, striking matches which
were handed round to light our tapers before we set out
into the dark streets in a procession of flickering lamps,
accompanying the statue of Jesus bearing the cross. The
following night in the church, a band of men in white
robes carefully lifted down the figure representing the
crucified Christ. They tenderly bathed and anointed
Him, before placing Him in the holy glass coffin,
which they then raised reverently onto their shoulders
to file once again through the village, their way lit by a
host of small fluttering flames.

Dark-eyed children walked slowly through the
freezing night, rugged up in beanies, ponchos and
scarves, clutching their candles flickering pink, blue or

green through the paper covers, every one with intricate individual cut-outs and decorations meticulously pasted on. Little faces glowed in the light, surrounded by young parents, aunties and uncles, grandparents and great-grandparents. I recognised the comfort and security they all drew from knowing they were a part of a protective whole ... and as we moved forward together, I felt it too. I kept my hand-crafted candle-holder to bring home as a memory of such an effort of love, offered up into the hands of a stranger.

When I returned to the hotel, I resisted the urge to secretly check the level of the wine cask.

Back in Arequipa for Easter Sunday, I beheld the effigy of Judas Iscariot hanging from a stone archway of the Plaza Yanahuara. It sported a silly grin and bore a strong resemblance to the current president of Peru ... or, for me, the whole of the hunger-striking staff of the Poder Judicial rolled into one. A satirical speech had already begun, and railed on for more than thirty minutes, poking fun and heaping blame on the disciple for the past year of idiocies and bungling, injustices and outrage, at national, regional and local level. As I listened and laughed, I thought maliciously of the bureaucrats who were frustrating progress in getting back our land.

Now came the moment the crowd of over a thousand had been waiting for, la Quema de Judas, the burning of the effigy, an annual Easter Sunday event. All of a sudden sparks spurted forth out of the clown's mouth and he began to fizz round and round, as more silver showers rushed out of his ears and nostrils. Then pouf! an arm exploded, followed closely by the other with a bang! as the brass band struck up. Next, a stream of light atoms arched out from an altogether different area, his penis, and once again he started spinning to hoots of laughter from the crowd ... round and round he went, spraying everyone with urine-coloured fireworks, as whoosh! off flew one leg. The opposite foot was by now revolving crazily just before the other limb blew up. The trumpets reached a crescendo as a barrage gust forth from the buttocks of the ragged remains, showering the crowd with heaven knows what. The torso whirled round violently until with an almighty blast it too erupted. Finally the head twisted, twirled, and shot off ... and all that remained of the annoyances, sorrows, frustrations and rotten luck of the previous year, amounted to a few puffs of smoke and some threads hanging from a metal frame. Moments later, municipal employees moved in to dismantle it, and I walked home grinning as I thought of the Poder Judicial and the hilarious scene I'd just witnessed.

Celebrations continued through the afternoon with the sharing of the traditional meal of thirteen courses representing Jesus and his disciples, at my landlady's elegant home. Settling into the easy chatter and warmth of her extended family visiting from Cusco, I began with chupe de camarones, the exquisite shrimp soup of the region, progressed on to quinua pancakes and finally the traditional Easter fruit jelly, mazamorra … with a lot more in between. That prediction all those years ago on a bushwalk in Tasmania did not apply only to my birthday.

CHAPTER 35

Rosa and the staff chose a $40 locally-produced, high-quality set of books with CD for all levels of primary language studies for children's use at home and at school. About half the parents paid; the rest unable or unwilling, meaning their children would miss out on many classroom activities. Upset by this injustice, I used funds from friends in Australia to make up the shortfall. We tried to overcome the issue of parental jealousy, by extracting a commitment from the poorest to contribute one sol per day to repay the debt. Even so, some, we knew, would never pay a centavo, which wouldn't have mattered at all … if only the other children in the class hadn't known too and reported back to their families. As I handed a book to a destitute boy in Grade 1, the girl opposite him said with surprising spite, 'His mother won't pay for that. She's got no money. How come he gets the book?' I knew she was merely repeating what she'd heard at home, but it sounded depressingly ugly coming from a six year old.

Another member of the same class who would never have acquired a textbook without help was Pamela's son, Rafael. I'd first met him as a two year old with sodden pants lying asleep on the bed in her shack. Following the poisoning incident and his months in foster care – with whatever did or didn't happen there – he'd returned home and started kindergarten at Colegio Elohim. By Grade 1, he presented as a highly intelligent, winning child, responsible and eager to help, despite some moments of stubborn rebellion. He had two younger siblings, his mother, tubes still untied, due to give birth again any minute to her eighth baby … and his oldest sister Veronica, to her first, pregnant at fifteen as predicted to the married combi driver.

By now able to accept my complete lack of control over these outcomes, I did decide that I could at least do something when I spied Rafael flopping around in shoes without socks or laces. I went to the market and spent $3 on the necessary items. The next day, after some hauling, threading and tying of bows, Rafael bunny-hopped out of the classroom and spent the morning break running and jumping around, grinning from ear to ear.

Over the week, I sought him out regularly to pull up the socks and tie the laces, until one afternoon he left school in his shoes but returned in broken sandals the next morning. He avoided me and there was no point in causing him stress by asking him what had happened – they'd clearly been lost somewhere in Pamela's shack. At least his feet had been comfortable for a short time.

The same week, I arrived for the annual Mother's Day concert, finding preparations at fever pitch, the children already having struggled into their hired dance costumes, dresses and suits. Little girls lined up to have make-up expertly applied by mothers in tracksuits with sleeping bundles on their backs and grubby toddlers in tow, to highlight their daughters' huge dark eyes and high cheekbones. I stood admiring gorgeous satin dresses, adorned lashes, eyelids and lips, lustrous braids and beads, and thick, ribboned plaits; while the boys sported gelled hair, brilliant shoes to match, ponchos and straw sombreros … when came a call, 'Mees Soosi, please come and help!' I found myself with a comb in my hand, faced with a head of long, black locks, which I had to plait, wind and adorn with a rose for a small performer. The plaits I could manage, just, but hair braiding and decorating had never counted among my talents. I twisted the dark tresses this way and that, nervously watching the pretty little face grimace as I pulled too hard, finally sticking in the rose and sending her on her way to dance, calling helpfully after her, 'Don't move too much!'

Later I held my breath as her class performed the

marinera. She swirled her long skirt and dipped her head gracefully – the rose, and her hair, staying put.

After the performances, I delivered a short speech of thanks to staff and parents for a gift. Moments later, Rafael sidled up to me, his eyes bereft, his top lip quivering. 'Mees Soosi, are you leaving and never coming back?'

As his grubby, serious little face stared earnestly into mine, I thought of Pamela's continuing supply of vulnerable children and how they strengthened my sense of purpose here in Arequipa.

'Don't worry, Rafaelito,' I said cheerfully, 'I'll be back on Monday.'

Some weeks later, Paulo turned up unexpectedly at Colegio Elohim. He had left us four years earlier, and when our attempts to help him enrol in secondary school had failed, he had found work as a combi conductor, which at least ensured him a midday meal on his shifts. But his mother had died of alcoholism shortly afterwards and the last we'd heard he'd been roaming with a street gang. I sat with Rosa in her office beside this abandoned boy, now sixteen. Head bowed, he whispered that he had nowhere to sleep except in the hovel with his father and brothers, all addicted as his mother had been. I recalled our visit and asked him if he'd been drinking with them.

'Yes,' he said and in a halting voice explained he wanted to change, and asked if we could help him apply for a technical secondary course in town.

'So you have made the decision,' said Rosa, 'that you're going to be different?'

Paulo glanced up and a tear rolled down his cheek.

Rosa continued, 'We'll see if we can find the registration fee and a room for you. But you must promise to keep up with your studies.'

As we walked to the gate, he hugged me and mumbled, 'Gracias, Mees Soosi.'

With a lump in my throat I replied, 'Paolito, it's a pleasure. Come and see us soon, so we can organise things.'

The following week, as I ran for the combi at the marketplace, a male voice called out to me, and I saw Paulo, the conductor, hanging out of another vehicle slowing to a stop. I raced over to greet him and he said, 'I'll come up to Elohim soon.'

'We're waiting for you.'

That same day, Rosa told me that Paulo's eighteen-year-old brother, also an ex-student, had just been hauled off to jail for assaulting a man and stealing his cell phone. She'd heard he didn't do it, just happened to be nearby, scruffy and drunk at the time, pounced on by the police after a tip-off from nosey neighbours.

I had no illusions about what might happen to Paulo.

He might not return, lured away by alcohol or crime from his dream of graduating to study heavy-machinery operation. I could only wait and hope … and reflect that if our construction had proceeded offering technical training options for him and his brother, things might have been different.

The auction process was going nowhere. The strike at the Poder Judicial had finally ended, and nobody had starved, but the backlog of work brought no guarantee that our case might be heard that year, the following year, or ten years hence. We'd come so close, only to have it snatched from our grasp.

My six tourist months in Peru were almost up. Frustrated at the land situation, I decided to return to Australia via Boston. I had enough money thanks to rent from the Sydney apartment, and I'd finally given up feeling guilty over my extreme fortune in being able to travel to the first world to recharge my batteries.

Three weeks before leaving, I went with Antonio for a final weekend back to Yanque in Colca Canyon, this time to stay in a small local hotel right in the village. We explored stone ruins, soaked once again in thermal hot springs, danced with the locals around an evening bonfire, and joined them for mass in the colonial church.

The most intense images which remain etched in my memory, however, were of his telltale agitation over dinner on the Saturday evening, and of him sitting later on his bed in the dark secretly scoffing long draughts of pisco disguised in a water bottle after he thought I'd gone to sleep.

When he finally stretched out and I heard his even breathing, I sat up, eyes wide and dry. After all the years of misgivings, doubt and mistrust, this was the first absolute, irrefutable proof of what had been going on, what he'd been keeping from me. All those behaviours I recognised but couldn't explain – here at last, the reason stared me belligerently in the face.

Wrapped in a blanket, I scrawled a note to him by torchlight, feeling almost relieved that it had come to a head. I wrote that I'd finally realised my own guilt in allowing him to have it all and live a lie between his beloved gringa during the day and his equally beloved pisco at night. I couldn't change his actions but I could change mine. I finished the letter, placed it under the half-empty water bottle and lay down, silence pressing on my ears in the night gloom. I shuddered and pulled up the covers. It could be denied no longer. The storm-clouds which had unleashed such destruction at every level of our school community had finally rolled onto my own horizon.

We spoke little the following morning and caught the bus back to our separate homes at midday. I immediately went online and ordered the story of the co-founder of Alcoholics Anonymous, written by his wife. Over two days, I hardly moved from my desk, following her unflinching account of their struggle with his addiction. As I stopped from time to time to contemplate my garden, I sensed that reading this book was probably one of the most important things I would ever do.

Two quotes jumped out at me, the first, 'I did love him, but I was enabling him to drink because there were no consequences with me and he knew it,' and the second, 'the spouses of alcoholics (are) such warm and wonderful enablers.' I wasn't sure whether I still loved Antonio, and I certainly didn't consider myself warm or wonderful, but I knew I cared enough for him, and for myself, to begin accepting some responsibility.

For two weeks we had no contact. The day before I left, stopping by his flat, I found him unable to meet my eyes, distant and sad. He said he did not want to discuss the matter and that he would take his own measures. Handing over details of AA, its twelve steps, and information on meditation and relaxation, I didn't mention hope, misery, love or expectations; and neither did he. We walked to the bus stop and hugged briefly before I climbed aboard and found a seat at the back.

He stood still, his shoulders slumped, as my combi pulled away.

Late that afternoon, at my kitchen window, I shivered as the sun retreated from the garden and a chill breeze rustled the delicate yellowing leaves of the jacaranda. Glancing upward, I spotted the turquoise hummingbird perched on the top branch to catch the last rays. It swung its beak from side to side, chattering its farewell to another day before the onset of cold darkness.

The following afternoon I would fly out for Boston and then Sydney. I'd tidied the cottage so Greta could stay there during her visit from Sweden. Beyond the five months away, the vast unknown which lay ahead defied any attempt at planning. Would we ever be able to buy the land so desperately needed for Colegio Elohim? And Antonio? His stricken face appeared before me and I blinked back tears. The little bird stopped turning its head and stared down at me sideways. I took a deep breath and gazed back.

CHAPTER 36

Boston welcomed me, decked out with harvest wreaths and window boxes planted in dazzling autumn colours. I roamed markets which were bursting with sunflowers, pumpkins and home-baked cranberry pies, boogied at the Bean Town Jazz Festival, visited theatres, author talks and art studios, even joined in a fun run down the river. I felt as if disentangling myself from Arequipa and taking off had begun a roll-on effect.

A call came on Skype from Antonio just days after I'd left Peru. 'I've survived my first twenty-four hours without a drink,' he announced. 'I slept like a baby and this morning I remembered everything.' He'd studied the list I'd left him, found a group, and been to an AA meeting. I couldn't believe it and reminded myself that it was early days yet. In regular communication over the following months, he continued to promise he had not given in to his old temptress, as he gradually admitted the secret life he'd been leading.

One of AA's 'twelve steps' of recovery is an undertaking to 'make amends' to those who have been hurt by the drinker's behaviour. Antonio fulfilled this pledge by giving me permission to write this account.

While staying with friends in Australia, I decided that within twelve months I'd move into my new apartment and set it up as short-lease furnished accommodation. This would mean that during future travels I'd have a Sydney home base for the first time in many years.

The roll continued as I finally fulfilled a goal I'd set myself while waiting on that deserted Sydney suburban train platform on Christmas Day exactly three years earlier. Having celebrated with my brother the previous week, I joined in a family afternoon on December 25th with the children, including Rachel visiting from Berlin, plus Richard, his mother, and his siblings. Although his wife did not come, we'd taken a first step.

For all that, though, after the event, which I'd longed for and had gone so smoothly, I was overcome with sadness. I tried to rationalise myself out of it – he had a new life, so did I, everyone had moved on. But what about the twenty-odd years we'd shared raising a family; did that count for nothing? A wise companion put her finger on the feeling – a sense of loss – one that would always remain. Once I'd named it, I found

I could accept it, even invite it to stay and welcome it into the complex treasure of emotions, experiences and lessons which makes up my soul.

At 9 am on January 21st, after a night of bucketing rain, I awoke to rainbow lorikeets screeching across a freshly-painted blue Sydney sky. I was surprised that I had slept late because on that day I expected news of the auction for Colegio Elohim's embargoed land. At the beginning of the month, a date had finally been published, and it should have taken place in Arequipa at 2 am that very morning Australian time. I took nothing for granted, though, and would believe it only when I heard or read it. I took a deep breath and opened my email. Nothing. Rosa had promised to send a message the minute it happened. I grabbed my mobile and punched in her number … and for once she answered.

'Rosa, what's happening?' I asked, straining to listen as the cicadas started up outside the window. She said almost word for word what we'd been waiting to hear for two years.

'We bought the land … at reserve price … No other bidders … We own it now. Gracias a Dios!'

Later that morning, I stood in the park beneath the Harbour Bridge before a gentle chop of blue water and the shining white Opera House sails beyond. I rang Antonio, who I hoped would have just arrived home from his last evening class. He picked up immediately and I broke the news, laughing and jigging in the summer sunshine. Suddenly, I wanted more than anything to get back to Arequipa. I didn't know what awaited me there, but I began counting the days until I'd cross the sea again to find out.

EPILOGUE

Patricia stands before us in her pyjamas, dressing gown, slippers and the string of pearls she never takes off. Beneath the rotunda in her garden, our group of four is braving the soggy chill of a misty Arequipa morning. Tall and balanced at seventy-six, she leads us in Tai Chi, as she has every day since I've been back.

'Make a circle with your arms in front of you,' she says. 'Contemplate your own life within the emptiness … all its opportunities and its restraints. Bring to your heart a sense of gratefulness for what you are.'

I stare at my clasped fingers and take a deep breath.

'Embrace your tiger and make a "yes" of all your moments. Return to mountain.'

I separate and lower my hands, pushing them down by my sides. This confirms acceptance of the place where I belong in the broader context of creation. I have an individual life, my 'tiger' which I've embraced, and I have a specific spot in a greater universe, my 'mountain'.

At Colegio Elohim, construction is already under-way on the newly-purchased land. The school term has begun, the current working classrooms insulated from the bedlam next door. Antonio tells me he's sleeping better and can remember everything as he continues free of pisco. We still meet for Sunday lunch and some-times a brief dinner during the week, and for now it is enough, as we assess the depths of the damage between us.

Patricia rests, her arms hanging, relaxed.

'You are part of a puzzle. It is vast, but without you, it is not complete. You were created for a purpose and if you can find your shape and dissolve your small ego, you will fit perfectly.'

I ponder the past ten years and everything that's hap-pened while my body moves again to embrace its tiger, return to its mountain.

'In spite of the contradictions you endure, you can live a balanced life, totally integrated in mind, heart, body and spirit.'

A subtle fusion has taken hold in my soul, of moti-vation to 'do' and faith in 'not doing'. My ideas for the future in Arequipa, in Sydney and beyond form an ethereal string of possibilities which may happen and, of course, may not. Things will come to their own bal-ance if I let them.

'Embrace tiger, return to mountain.'

As I repeat the movement, I notice a sodden, dark-crimson rose drooping low on its stalk, petals glistening with droplets in a shaft of weak grey light. A realisation dawns. This book, which began in Sydney's sunshine more than ten years ago, will finish here in the gentle rain of a garden on the other side of the Pacific.

'Accept yourself within the boundaries you choose and you can be free, knowing you belong to a larger picture.'

My experiences in Nepal and Rwanda set me on the road to find freedom in Peru. I have finally come to understand and welcome my place. As I move through the mist to Tai Chi, I see a little girl toddling in the darkness long ago on the London Road. She crossed the globe once to become a woman, marry and raise a family of her own. By and by, her restless soul took her off again and she found other children and other adults, adapting her perspective along the way. I'll continue down this path wherever it guides me for as long as I can within the time I'm granted.

'If you can be present to your limitations and possibilities and live to the fullest within your reality, your spirit can frolic joyfully in the spaciousness you own.'

While all around me, hummingbirds dance.

ACKNOWLEDGEMENTS

In writing these pages I have been inspired by the influence, both positive and negative, but always fascinating, of the multitude of souls who crossed my path ... hence the dedication at the beginning of the book. Nonetheless, I would like to offer up some special, individual words of appreciation.

To my publisher, Rod Morrison, for his highly perceptive commentaries and suggestions, always delivered with infinite tact and unfailing patience. To Annabel Blay for her part in the process. And to Jon MacDonald for designing a cover which perfectly reflects the essence of my life in Arequipa.

To my Peruvian partner, my Australian ex-husband and my four children, for reading and approving the 'bits about them' ... and to my son and oldest daughter who reviewed the whole manuscript in its early stages and produced helpful feedback. To the other 'test readers', Sophie Mirkva, Michèle Darling, Malcolm

Pearce and Susan Peryman, who gave their precious time and considerable expertise to read the work and deliver invaluable advice. I am deeply grateful to you all.

To Susanne Gervay for her unfailing support and enthusiasm, and Janet Fennell for her inspiring creative writing courses.

To Patricia Roberts and Malcolm Pearce for their spiritual guidance which has continued over a decade, on both sides of the Pacific.

To María Rosa Gil Huamán for sharing her life, her dream, and her unswerving faith.

To the writers of the books, articles and reviews, in particular *The Lois Wilson Story, When Love Is Not Enough* by William G. Borchert (Hazelden, 2010); *Buddhism for Busy People* by David Michie (Snow Lion, 2008); *Demasiados héroes* by Laura Restrepo (Alfaguara, 2009); and 'Not Dwelling Anywhere', from *Sacred Journey, Journal of Fellowship in Prayer* Vol. 63, No. 3 by Florence Caplow, which have shaped my thinking and from which I have gratefully quoted.

And to the children of Colegio Elohim, who have given me so much more than they will ever know. All proceeds from the sale of this memoir will go towards their continuing 'empowerment through education'.

For more details, please visit:

www.elohimarequipa.org

Lightning Source UK Ltd.
Milton Keynes UK
UKHW041812030219
336574UK00013B/223/P